C-3724   CAREER EXAMINATION SERIES

This is your
PASSBOOK for...

Income Maintenance Supervisor

Test Preparation Study Guide
Questions & Answers

COPYRIGHT NOTICE

This book is SOLELY intended for, is sold ONLY to, and its use is RESTRICTED to individual, bona fide applicants or candidates who qualify by virtue of having seriously filed applications for appropriate license, certificate, professional and/or promotional advancement, higher school matriculation, scholarship, or other legitimate requirements of education and/or governmental authorities.

This book is NOT intended for use, class instruction, tutoring, training, duplication, copying, reprinting, excerption, or adaptation, etc., by:

1) Other publishers
2) Proprietors and/or Instructors of "Coaching" and/or Preparatory Courses
3) Personnel and/or Training Divisions of commercial, industrial, and governmental organizations
4) Schools, colleges, or universities and/or their departments and staffs, including teachers and other personnel
5) Testing Agencies or Bureaus
6) Study groups which seek by the purchase of a single volume to copy and/or duplicate and/or adapt this material for use by the group as a whole without having purchased individual volumes for each of the members of the group
7) Et al.

Such persons would be in violation of appropriate Federal and State statutes.

PROVISION OF LICENSING AGREEMENTS – Recognized educational, commercial, industrial, and governmental institutions and organizations, and others legitimately engaged in educational pursuits, including training, testing, and measurement activities, may address request for a licensing agreement to the copyright owners, who will determine whether, and under what conditions, including fees and charges, the materials in this book may be used them. In other words, a licensing facility exists for the legitimate use of the material in this book on other than an individual basis. However, it is asseverated and affirmed here that the material in this book CANNOT be used without the receipt of the express permission of such a licensing agreement from the Publishers. Inquiries re licensing should be addressed to the company, attention rights and permissions department.

All rights reserved, including the right of reproduction in whole or in part, in any form or by any means, electronic or mechanical, including photocopying, recording, or by any information storage and retrieval system, without permission in writing from the Publisher.

Copyright © 2025 by
National Learning Corporation

212 Michael Drive, Syosset, NY 11791
(516) 921-8888 • www.passbooks.com
E-mail: info@passbooks.com

PASSBOOK® SERIES

THE *PASSBOOK® SERIES* has been created to prepare applicants and candidates for the ultimate academic battlefield – the examination room.

At some time in our lives, each and every one of us may be required to take an examination – for validation, matriculation, admission, qualification, registration, certification, or licensure.

Based on the assumption that every applicant or candidate has met the basic formal educational standards, has taken the required number of courses, and read the necessary texts, the *PASSBOOK® SERIES* furnishes the one special preparation which may assure passing with confidence, instead of failing with insecurity. Examination questions – together with answers – are furnished as the basic vehicle for study so that the mysteries of the examination and its compounding difficulties may be eliminated or diminished by a sure method.

This book is meant to help you pass your examination provided that you qualify and are serious in your objective.

The entire field is reviewed through the huge store of content information which is succinctly presented through a provocative and challenging approach – the question-and-answer method.

A climate of success is established by furnishing the correct answers at the end of each test.

You soon learn to recognize types of questions, forms of questions, and patterns of questioning. You may even begin to anticipate expected outcomes.

You perceive that many questions are repeated or adapted so that you can gain acute insights, which may enable you to score many sure points.

You learn how to confront new questions, or types of questions, and to attack them confidently and work out the correct answers.

You note objectives and emphases, and recognize pitfalls and dangers, so that you may make positive educational adjustments.

Moreover, you are kept fully informed in relation to new concepts, methods, practices, and directions in the field.

You discover that you are actually taking the examination all the time: you are preparing for the examination by "taking" an examination, not by reading extraneous and/or supererogatory textbooks.

In short, this PASSBOOK®, used directedly, should be an important factor in helping you to pass your test.

INCOME MAINTENANCE SUPERVISOR

DUTIES
Supervises and assists in planning and coordinating the activities of a group of Income Maintenance Workers and assigned para-professional staff; assists in organizing assigned work and supervises the work activities of a group of Income Maintenance Workers; assists in planning and conducting staff meetings of policy and procedures; analyzes, comprehends and interprets laws, rules, regulations and policies regarding financial eligibility and applies them with reasonable consistency; supervises the maintenance of essential records and files; prepares suitable reports; makes appraisals and evaluations of the work efficiency of individual staff members and of the quality of the professional service provided by the income maintenance staff; does related work as required.

SCOPE OF THE WRITTEN TEST
The written test will be designed to test for knowledge, skills, and/or abilities in such areas as:
1. Laws, rules and regulations related to financial eligibility and income maintenance;
2. Current issues, policies and problems in administering social service programs;
3. Understanding and interpreting written material based on social services related material;
4. Arithmetic computation;
5. Preparing written material; and
6. Supervision.

HOW TO TAKE A TEST

I. YOU MUST PASS AN EXAMINATION

A. *WHAT EVERY CANDIDATE SHOULD KNOW*

Examination applicants often ask us for help in preparing for the written test. What can I study in advance? What kinds of questions will be asked? How will the test be given? How will the papers be graded?

As an applicant for a civil service examination, you may be wondering about some of these things. Our purpose here is to suggest effective methods of advance study and to describe civil service examinations.

Your chances for success on this examination can be increased if you know how to prepare. Those "pre-examination jitters" can be reduced if you know what to expect. You can even experience an adventure in good citizenship if you know why civil service exams are given.

B. *WHY ARE CIVIL SERVICE EXAMINATIONS GIVEN?*

Civil service examinations are important to you in two ways. As a citizen, you want public jobs filled by employees who know how to do their work. As a job seeker, you want a fair chance to compete for that job on an equal footing with other candidates. The best-known means of accomplishing this two-fold goal is the competitive examination.

Exams are widely publicized throughout the nation. They may be administered for jobs in federal, state, city, municipal, town or village governments or agencies.

Any citizen may apply, with some limitations, such as the age or residence of applicants. Your experience and education may be reviewed to see whether you meet the requirements for the particular examination. When these requirements exist, they are reasonable and applied consistently to all applicants. Thus, a competitive examination may cause you some uneasiness now, but it is your privilege and safeguard.

C. *HOW ARE CIVIL SERVICE EXAMS DEVELOPED?*

Examinations are carefully written by trained technicians who are specialists in the field known as "psychological measurement," in consultation with recognized authorities in the field of work that the test will cover. These experts recommend the subject matter areas or skills to be tested; only those knowledges or skills important to your success on the job are included. The most reliable books and source materials available are used as references. Together, the experts and technicians judge the difficulty level of the questions.

Test technicians know how to phrase questions so that the problem is clearly stated. Their ethics do not permit "trick" or "catch" questions. Questions may have been tried out on sample groups, or subjected to statistical analysis, to determine their usefulness.

Written tests are often used in combination with performance tests, ratings of training and experience, and oral interviews. All of these measures combine to form the best-known means of finding the right person for the right job.

II. HOW TO PASS THE WRITTEN TEST

A. NATURE OF THE EXAMINATION

To prepare intelligently for civil service examinations, you should know how they differ from school examinations you have taken. In school you were assigned certain definite pages to read or subjects to cover. The examination questions were quite detailed and usually emphasized memory. Civil service exams, on the other hand, try to discover your present ability to perform the duties of a position, plus your potentiality to learn these duties. In other words, a civil service exam attempts to predict how successful you will be. Questions cover such a broad area that they cannot be as minute and detailed as school exam questions.

In the public service similar kinds of work, or positions, are grouped together in one "class." This process is known as *position-classification*. All the positions in a class are paid according to the salary range for that class. One class title covers all of these positions, and they are all tested by the same examination.

B. FOUR BASIC STEPS

1) Study the announcement

How, then, can you know what subjects to study? Our best answer is: "Learn as much as possible about the class of positions for which you've applied." The exam will test the knowledge, skills and abilities needed to do the work.

Your most valuable source of information about the position you want is the official exam announcement. This announcement lists the training and experience qualifications. Check these standards and apply only if you come reasonably close to meeting them.

The brief description of the position in the examination announcement offers some clues to the subjects which will be tested. Think about the job itself. Review the duties in your mind. Can you perform them, or are there some in which you are rusty? Fill in the blank spots in your preparation.

Many jurisdictions preview the written test in the exam announcement by including a section called "Knowledge and Abilities Required," "Scope of the Examination," or some similar heading. Here you will find out specifically what fields will be tested.

2) Review your own background

Once you learn in general what the position is all about, and what you need to know to do the work, ask yourself which subjects you already know fairly well and which need improvement. You may wonder whether to concentrate on improving your strong areas or on building some background in your fields of weakness. When the announcement has specified "some knowledge" or "considerable knowledge," or has used adjectives like "beginning principles of…" or "advanced … methods," you can get a clue as to the number and difficulty of questions to be asked in any given field. More questions, and hence broader coverage, would be included for those subjects which are more important in the work. Now weigh your strengths and weaknesses against the job requirements and prepare accordingly.

3) Determine the level of the position

Another way to tell how intensively you should prepare is to understand the level of the job for which you are applying. Is it the entering level? In other words, is this the position in which beginners in a field of work are hired? Or is it an intermediate or advanced level? Sometimes this is indicated by such words as "Junior" or "Senior" in the class title. Other jurisdictions use Roman numerals to designate the level – Clerk I, Clerk II, for example. The word "Supervisor" sometimes appears in the title. If the level is not indicated by the title, check the description of duties. Will you be working under very close supervision, or will you have responsibility for independent decisions in this work?

4) Choose appropriate study materials

Now that you know the subjects to be examined and the relative amount of each subject to be covered, you can choose suitable study materials. For beginning level jobs, or even advanced ones, if you have a pronounced weakness in some aspect of your training, read a modern, standard textbook in that field. Be sure it is up to date and has general coverage. Such books are normally available at your library, and the librarian will be glad to help you locate one. For entry-level positions, questions of appropriate difficulty are chosen – neither highly advanced questions, nor those too simple. Such questions require careful thought but not advanced training.

If the position for which you are applying is technical or advanced, you will read more advanced, specialized material. If you are already familiar with the basic principles of your field, elementary textbooks would waste your time. Concentrate on advanced textbooks and technical periodicals. Think through the concepts and review difficult problems in your field.

These are all general sources. You can get more ideas on your own initiative, following these leads. For example, training manuals and publications of the government agency which employs workers in your field can be useful, particularly for technical and professional positions. A letter or visit to the government department involved may result in more specific study suggestions, and certainly will provide you with a more definite idea of the exact nature of the position you are seeking.

III. KINDS OF TESTS

Tests are used for purposes other than measuring knowledge and ability to perform specified duties. For some positions, it is equally important to test ability to make adjustments to new situations or to profit from training. In others, basic mental abilities not dependent on information are essential. Questions which test these things may not appear as pertinent to the duties of the position as those which test for knowledge and information. Yet they are often highly important parts of a fair examination. For very general questions, it is almost impossible to help you direct your study efforts. What we can do is to point out some of the more common of these general abilities needed in public service positions and describe some typical questions.

1) General information

Broad, general information has been found useful for predicting job success in some kinds of work. This is tested in a variety of ways, from vocabulary lists to questions about current events. Basic background in some field of work, such as sociology or economics, may be sampled in a group of questions. Often these are principles which have become familiar to most persons through exposure rather than through formal training. It is difficult to advise you how to study for these questions; being alert to the world around you is our best suggestion.

2) Verbal ability

An example of an ability needed in many positions is verbal or language ability. Verbal ability is, in brief, the ability to use and understand words. Vocabulary and grammar tests are typical measures of this ability. Reading comprehension or paragraph interpretation questions are common in many kinds of civil service tests. You are given a paragraph of written material and asked to find its central meaning.

3) Numerical ability

Number skills can be tested by the familiar arithmetic problem, by checking paired lists of numbers to see which are alike and which are different, or by interpreting charts and graphs. In the latter test, a graph may be printed in the test booklet which you are asked to use as the basis for answering questions.

4) Observation

A popular test for law-enforcement positions is the observation test. A picture is shown to you for several minutes, then taken away. Questions about the picture test your ability to observe both details and larger elements.

5) Following directions

In many positions in the public service, the employee must be able to carry out written instructions dependably and accurately. You may be given a chart with several columns, each column listing a variety of information. The questions require you to carry out directions involving the information given in the chart.

6) Skills and aptitudes

Performance tests effectively measure some manual skills and aptitudes. When the skill is one in which you are trained, such as typing or shorthand, you can practice. These tests are often very much like those given in business school or high school courses. For many of the other skills and aptitudes, however, no short-time preparation can be made. Skills and abilities natural to you or that you have developed throughout your lifetime are being tested.

Many of the general questions just described provide all the data needed to answer the questions and ask you to use your reasoning ability to find the answers. Your best preparation for these tests, as well as for tests of facts and ideas, is to be at your physical and mental best. You, no doubt, have your own methods of getting into an exam-taking mood and keeping "in shape." The next section lists some ideas on this subject.

IV. KINDS OF QUESTIONS

Only rarely is the "essay" question, which you answer in narrative form, used in civil service tests. Civil service tests are usually of the short-answer type. Full instructions for answering these questions will be given to you at the examination. But in case this is your first experience with short-answer questions and separate answer sheets, here is what you need to know:

1) Multiple-choice Questions

Most popular of the short-answer questions is the "multiple choice" or "best answer" question. It can be used, for example, to test for factual knowledge, ability to solve problems or judgment in meeting situations found at work.

A multiple-choice question is normally one of three types—
- It can begin with an incomplete statement followed by several possible endings. You are to find the one ending which *best* completes the statement, although some of the others may not be entirely wrong.
- It can also be a complete statement in the form of a question which is answered by choosing one of the statements listed.

- It can be in the form of a problem – again you select the best answer.

Here is an example of a multiple-choice question with a discussion which should give you some clues as to the method for choosing the right answer:

When an employee has a complaint about his assignment, the action which will *best* help him overcome his difficulty is to
- A. discuss his difficulty with his coworkers
- B. take the problem to the head of the organization
- C. take the problem to the person who gave him the assignment
- D. say nothing to anyone about his complaint

In answering this question, you should study each of the choices to find which is best. Consider choice "A" – Certainly an employee may discuss his complaint with fellow employees, but no change or improvement can result, and the complaint remains unresolved. Choice "B" is a poor choice since the head of the organization probably does not know what assignment you have been given, and taking your problem to him is known as "going over the head" of the supervisor. The supervisor, or person who made the assignment, is the person who can clarify it or correct any injustice. Choice "C" is, therefore, correct. To say nothing, as in choice "D," is unwise. Supervisors have and interest in knowing the problems employees are facing, and the employee is seeking a solution to his problem.

2) True/False Questions

The "true/false" or "right/wrong" form of question is sometimes used. Here a complete statement is given. Your job is to decide whether the statement is right or wrong.

SAMPLE: A roaming cell-phone call to a nearby city costs less than a non-roaming call to a distant city.

This statement is wrong, or false, since roaming calls are more expensive.

This is not a complete list of all possible question forms, although most of the others are variations of these common types. You will always get complete directions for answering questions. Be sure you understand *how* to mark your answers – ask questions until you do.

V. RECORDING YOUR ANSWERS

Computer terminals are used more and more today for many different kinds of exams.

For an examination with very few applicants, you may be told to record your answers in the test booklet itself. Separate answer sheets are much more common. If this separate answer sheet is to be scored by machine – and this is often the case – it is highly important that you mark your answers correctly in order to get credit.

An electronic scoring machine is often used in civil service offices because of the speed with which papers can be scored. Machine-scored answer sheets must be marked with a pencil, which will be given to you. This pencil has a high graphite content which responds to the electronic scoring machine. As a matter of fact, stray dots may register as answers, so do not let your pencil rest on the answer sheet while you are pondering the correct answer. Also, if your pencil lead breaks or is otherwise defective, ask for another.

Since the answer sheet will be dropped in a slot in the scoring machine, be careful not to bend the corners or get the paper crumpled.

The answer sheet normally has five vertical columns of numbers, with 30 numbers to a column. These numbers correspond to the question numbers in your test booklet. After each number, going across the page are four or five pairs of dotted lines. These short dotted lines have small letters or numbers above them. The first two pairs may also have a "T" or "F" above the letters. This indicates that the first two pairs only are to be used if the questions are of the true-false type. If the questions are multiple choice, disregard the "T" and "F" and pay attention only to the small letters or numbers.

Answer your questions in the manner of the sample that follows:

    32. The largest city in the United States is
        A. Washington, D.C.
        B. New York City
        C. Chicago
        D. Detroit
        E. San Francisco

1) Choose the answer you think is best. (New York City is the largest, so "B" is correct.)
2) Find the row of dotted lines numbered the same as the question you are answering. (Find row number 32)
3) Find the pair of dotted lines corresponding to the answer. (Find the pair of lines under the mark "B.")
4) Make a solid black mark between the dotted lines.

VI. BEFORE THE TEST

Common sense will help you find procedures to follow to get ready for an examination. Too many of us, however, overlook these sensible measures. Indeed, nervousness and fatigue have been found to be the most serious reasons why applicants fail to do their best on civil service tests. Here is a list of reminders:

- Begin your preparation early – Don't wait until the last minute to go scurrying around for books and materials or to find out what the position is all about.
- Prepare continuously – An hour a night for a week is better than an all-night cram session. This has been definitely established. What is more, a night a week for a month will return better dividends than crowding your study into a shorter period of time.
- Locate the place of the exam – You have been sent a notice telling you when and where to report for the examination. If the location is in a different town or otherwise unfamiliar to you, it would be well to inquire the best route and learn something about the building.
- Relax the night before the test – Allow your mind to rest. Do not study at all that night. Plan some mild recreation or diversion; then go to bed early and get a good night's sleep.
- Get up early enough to make a leisurely trip to the place for the test – This way unforeseen events, traffic snarls, unfamiliar buildings, etc. will not upset you.
- Dress comfortably – A written test is not a fashion show. You will be known by number and not by name, so wear something comfortable.

- Leave excess paraphernalia at home – Shopping bags and odd bundles will get in your way. You need bring only the items mentioned in the official notice you received; usually everything you need is provided. Do not bring reference books to the exam. They will only confuse those last minutes and be taken away from you when in the test room.
- Arrive somewhat ahead of time – If because of transportation schedules you must get there very early, bring a newspaper or magazine to take your mind off yourself while waiting.
- Locate the examination room – When you have found the proper room, you will be directed to the seat or part of the room where you will sit. Sometimes you are given a sheet of instructions to read while you are waiting. Do not fill out any forms until you are told to do so; just read them and be prepared.
- Relax and prepare to listen to the instructions
- If you have any physical problem that may keep you from doing your best, be sure to tell the test administrator. If you are sick or in poor health, you really cannot do your best on the exam. You can come back and take the test some other time.

VII. AT THE TEST

The day of the test is here and you have the test booklet in your hand. The temptation to get going is very strong. Caution! There is more to success than knowing the right answers. You must know how to identify your papers and understand variations in the type of short-answer question used in this particular examination. Follow these suggestions for maximum results from your efforts:

1) Cooperate with the monitor

The test administrator has a duty to create a situation in which you can be as much at ease as possible. He will give instructions, tell you when to begin, check to see that you are marking your answer sheet correctly, and so on. He is not there to guard you, although he will see that your competitors do not take unfair advantage. He wants to help you do your best.

2) Listen to all instructions

Don't jump the gun! Wait until you understand all directions. In most civil service tests you get more time than you need to answer the questions. So don't be in a hurry. Read each word of instructions until you clearly understand the meaning. Study the examples, listen to all announcements and follow directions. Ask questions if you do not understand what to do.

3) Identify your papers

Civil service exams are usually identified by number only. You will be assigned a number; you must not put your name on your test papers. Be sure to copy your number correctly. Since more than one exam may be given, copy your exact examination title.

4) Plan your time

Unless you are told that a test is a "speed" or "rate of work" test, speed itself is usually not important. Time enough to answer all the questions will be provided, but this does not mean that you have all day. An overall time limit has been set. Divide the total time (in minutes) by the number of questions to determine the approximate time you have for each question.

5) Do not linger over difficult questions

If you come across a difficult question, mark it with a paper clip (useful to have along) and come back to it when you have been through the booklet. One caution if you do this – be sure to skip a number on your answer sheet as well. Check often to be sure that you have not lost your place and that you are marking in the row numbered the same as the question you are answering.

6) Read the questions

Be sure you know what the question asks! Many capable people are unsuccessful because they failed to *read* the questions correctly.

7) Answer all questions

Unless you have been instructed that a penalty will be deducted for incorrect answers, it is better to guess than to omit a question.

8) Speed tests

It is often better NOT to guess on speed tests. It has been found that on timed tests people are tempted to spend the last few seconds before time is called in marking answers at random – without even reading them – in the hope of picking up a few extra points. To discourage this practice, the instructions may warn you that your score will be "corrected" for guessing. That is, a penalty will be applied. The incorrect answers will be deducted from the correct ones, or some other penalty formula will be used.

9) Review your answers

If you finish before time is called, go back to the questions you guessed or omitted to give them further thought. Review other answers if you have time.

10) Return your test materials

If you are ready to leave before others have finished or time is called, take ALL your materials to the monitor and leave quietly. Never take any test material with you. The monitor can discover whose papers are not complete, and taking a test booklet may be grounds for disqualification.

VIII. EXAMINATION TECHNIQUES

1) Read the general instructions carefully. These are usually printed on the first page of the exam booklet. As a rule, these instructions refer to the timing of the examination; the fact that you should not start work until the signal and must stop work at a signal, etc. If there are any *special* instructions, such as a choice of questions to be answered, make sure that you note this instruction carefully.

2) When you are ready to start work on the examination, that is as soon as the signal has been given, read the instructions to each question booklet, underline any key words or phrases, such as *least, best, outline, describe* and the like. In this way you will tend to answer as requested rather than discover on reviewing your paper that you *listed without describing*, that you selected the *worst* choice rather than the *best* choice, etc.

3) If the examination is of the objective or multiple-choice type – that is, each question will also give a series of possible answers: A, B, C or D, and you are called upon to select the best answer and write the letter next to that answer on your answer paper – it is advisable to start answering each question in turn. There may be anywhere from 50 to 100 such questions in the three or four hours allotted and you can see how much time would be taken if you read through all the questions before beginning to answer any. Furthermore, if you come across a question or group of questions which you know would be difficult to answer, it would undoubtedly affect your handling of all the other questions.

4) If the examination is of the essay type and contains but a few questions, it is a moot point as to whether you should read all the questions before starting to answer any one. Of course, if you are given a choice – say five out of seven and the like – then it is essential to read all the questions so you can eliminate the two that are most difficult. If, however, you are asked to answer all the questions, there may be danger in trying to answer the easiest one first because you may find that you will spend too much time on it. The best technique is to answer the first question, then proceed to the second, etc.

5) Time your answers. Before the exam begins, write down the time it started, then add the time allowed for the examination and write down the time it must be completed, then divide the time available somewhat as follows:
    - If 3-1/2 hours are allowed, that would be 210 minutes. If you have 80 objective-type questions, that would be an average of 2-1/2 minutes per question. Allow yourself no more than 2 minutes per question, or a total of 160 minutes, which will permit about 50 minutes to review.
    - If for the time allotment of 210 minutes there are 7 essay questions to answer, that would average about 30 minutes a question. Give yourself only 25 minutes per question so that you have about 35 minutes to review.

6) The most important instruction is to *read each question* and make sure you know what is wanted. The second most important instruction is to *time yourself properly* so that you answer every question. The third most important instruction is to *answer every question*. Guess if you have to but include something for each question. Remember that you will receive no credit for a blank and will probably receive some credit if you write something in answer to an essay question. If you guess a letter – say "B" for a multiple-choice question – you may have guessed right. If you leave a blank as an answer to a multiple-choice question, the examiners may respect your feelings but it will not add a point to your score. Some exams may penalize you for wrong answers, so in such cases *only*, you may not want to guess unless you have some basis for your answer.

7) Suggestions
    a. Objective-type questions
        1. Examine the question booklet for proper sequence of pages and questions
        2. Read all instructions carefully
        3. Skip any question which seems too difficult; return to it after all other questions have been answered
        4. Apportion your time properly; do not spend too much time on any single question or group of questions

5. Note and underline key words – *all, most, fewest, least, best, worst, same, opposite,* etc.
6. Pay particular attention to negatives
7. Note unusual option, e.g., unduly long, short, complex, different or similar in content to the body of the question
8. Observe the use of "hedging" words – *probably, may, most likely,* etc.
9. Make sure that your answer is put next to the same number as the question
10. Do not second-guess unless you have good reason to believe the second answer is definitely more correct
11. Cross out original answer if you decide another answer is more accurate; do not erase until you are ready to hand your paper in
12. Answer all questions; guess unless instructed otherwise
13. Leave time for review

b. Essay questions
1. Read each question carefully
2. Determine exactly what is wanted. Underline key words or phrases.
3. Decide on outline or paragraph answer
4. Include many different points and elements unless asked to develop any one or two points or elements
5. Show impartiality by giving pros and cons unless directed to select one side only
6. Make and write down any assumptions you find necessary to answer the questions
7. Watch your English, grammar, punctuation and choice of words
8. Time your answers; don't crowd material

8) Answering the essay question

Most essay questions can be answered by framing the specific response around several key words or ideas. Here are a few such key words or ideas:

M's: manpower, materials, methods, money, management
P's: purpose, program, policy, plan, procedure, practice, problems, pitfalls, personnel, public relations

a. Six basic steps in handling problems:
1. Preliminary plan and background development
2. Collect information, data and facts
3. Analyze and interpret information, data and facts
4. Analyze and develop solutions as well as make recommendations
5. Prepare report and sell recommendations
6. Install recommendations and follow up effectiveness

b. Pitfalls to avoid
1. *Taking things for granted* – A statement of the situation does not necessarily imply that each of the elements is necessarily true; for example, a complaint may be invalid and biased so that all that can be taken for granted is that a complaint has been registered

2. *Considering only one side of a situation* – Wherever possible, indicate several alternatives and then point out the reasons you selected the best one
3. *Failing to indicate follow up* – Whenever your answer indicates action on your part, make certain that you will take proper follow-up action to see how successful your recommendations, procedures or actions turn out to be
4. *Taking too long in answering any single question* – Remember to time your answers properly

IX. AFTER THE TEST

Scoring procedures differ in detail among civil service jurisdictions although the general principles are the same. Whether the papers are hand-scored or graded by machine we have described, they are nearly always graded by number. That is, the person who marks the paper knows only the number – never the name – of the applicant. Not until all the papers have been graded will they be matched with names. If other tests, such as training and experience or oral interview ratings have been given, scores will be combined. Different parts of the examination usually have different weights. For example, the written test might count 60 percent of the final grade, and a rating of training and experience 40 percent. In many jurisdictions, veterans will have a certain number of points added to their grades.

After the final grade has been determined, the names are placed in grade order and an eligible list is established. There are various methods for resolving ties between those who get the same final grade – probably the most common is to place first the name of the person whose application was received first. Job offers are made from the eligible list in the order the names appear on it. You will be notified of your grade and your rank as soon as all these computations have been made. This will be done as rapidly as possible.

People who are found to meet the requirements in the announcement are called "eligibles." Their names are put on a list of eligible candidates. An eligible's chances of getting a job depend on how high he stands on this list and how fast agencies are filling jobs from the list.

When a job is to be filled from a list of eligibles, the agency asks for the names of people on the list of eligibles for that job. When the civil service commission receives this request, it sends to the agency the names of the three people highest on this list. Or, if the job to be filled has specialized requirements, the office sends the agency the names of the top three persons who meet these requirements from the general list.

The appointing officer makes a choice from among the three people whose names were sent to him. If the selected person accepts the appointment, the names of the others are put back on the list to be considered for future openings.

That is the rule in hiring from all kinds of eligible lists, whether they are for typist, carpenter, chemist, or something else. For every vacancy, the appointing officer has his choice of any one of the top three eligibles on the list. This explains why the person whose name is on top of the list sometimes does not get an appointment when some of the persons lower on the list do. If the appointing officer chooses the second or third eligible, the No. 1 eligible does not get a job at once, but stays on the list until he is appointed or the list is terminated.

X. HOW TO PASS THE INTERVIEW TEST

The examination for which you applied requires an oral interview test. You have already taken the written test and you are now being called for the interview test – the final part of the formal examination.

You may think that it is not possible to prepare for an interview test and that there are no procedures to follow during an interview. Our purpose is to point out some things you can do in advance that will help you and some good rules to follow and pitfalls to avoid while you are being interviewed.

What is an interview supposed to test?

The written examination is designed to test the technical knowledge and competence of the candidate; the oral is designed to evaluate intangible qualities, not readily measured otherwise, and to establish a list showing the relative fitness of each candidate – as measured against his competitors – for the position sought. Scoring is not on the basis of "right" and "wrong," but on a sliding scale of values ranging from "not passable" to "outstanding." As a matter of fact, it is possible to achieve a relatively low score without a single "incorrect" answer because of evident weakness in the qualities being measured.

Occasionally, an examination may consist entirely of an oral test – either an individual or a group oral. In such cases, information is sought concerning the technical knowledges and abilities of the candidate, since there has been no written examination for this purpose. More commonly, however, an oral test is used to supplement a written examination.

Who conducts interviews?

The composition of oral boards varies among different jurisdictions. In nearly all, a representative of the personnel department serves as chairman. One of the members of the board may be a representative of the department in which the candidate would work. In some cases, "outside experts" are used, and, frequently, a businessman or some other representative of the general public is asked to serve. Labor and management or other special groups may be represented. The aim is to secure the services of experts in the appropriate field.

However the board is composed, it is a good idea (and not at all improper or unethical) to ascertain in advance of the interview who the members are and what groups they represent. When you are introduced to them, you will have some idea of their backgrounds and interests, and at least you will not stutter and stammer over their names.

What should be done before the interview?

While knowledge about the board members is useful and takes some of the surprise element out of the interview, there is other preparation which is more substantive. It *is* possible to prepare for an oral interview – in several ways:

1) Keep a copy of your application and review it carefully before the interview

This may be the only document before the oral board, and the starting point of the interview. Know what education and experience you have listed there, and the sequence and dates of all of it. Sometimes the board will ask you to review the highlights of your experience for them; you should not have to hem and haw doing it.

2) Study the class specification and the examination announcement

Usually, the oral board has one or both of these to guide them. The qualities, characteristics or knowledges required by the position sought are stated in these documents. They offer valuable clues as to the nature of the oral interview. For example, if the job involves supervisory responsibilities, the announcement will usually indicate that knowledge of modern supervisory methods and the qualifications of the candidate as a supervisor will be tested. If so, you can expect such questions, frequently in the form of a hypothetical situation which you are expected to solve. NEVER go into an oral without knowledge of the duties and responsibilities of the job you seek.

3) Think through each qualification required

Try to visualize the kind of questions you would ask if you were a board member. How well could you answer them? Try especially to appraise your own knowledge and background in each area, *measured against the job sought*, and identify any areas in which you are weak. Be critical and realistic – do not flatter yourself.

4) Do some general reading in areas in which you feel you may be weak

For example, if the job involves supervision and your past experience has NOT, some general reading in supervisory methods and practices, particularly in the field of human relations, might be useful. Do NOT study agency procedures or detailed manuals. The oral board will be testing your understanding and capacity, not your memory.

5) Get a good night's sleep and watch your general health and mental attitude

You will want a clear head at the interview. Take care of a cold or any other minor ailment, and of course, no hangovers.

What should be done on the day of the interview?

Now comes the day of the interview itself. Give yourself plenty of time to get there. Plan to arrive somewhat ahead of the scheduled time, particularly if your appointment is in the fore part of the day. If a previous candidate fails to appear, the board might be ready for you a bit early. By early afternoon an oral board is almost invariably behind schedule if there are many candidates, and you may have to wait. Take along a book or magazine to read, or your application to review, but leave any extraneous material in the waiting room when you go in for your interview. In any event, relax and compose yourself.

The matter of dress is important. The board is forming impressions about you – from your experience, your manners, your attitude, and your appearance. Give your personal appearance careful attention. Dress your best, but not your flashiest. Choose conservative, appropriate clothing, and be sure it is immaculate. This is a business interview, and your appearance should indicate that you regard it as such. Besides, being well groomed and properly dressed will help boost your confidence.

Sooner or later, someone will call your name and escort you into the interview room. *This is it.* From here on you are on your own. It is too late for any more preparation. But remember, you asked for this opportunity to prove your fitness, and you are here because your request was granted.

What happens when you go in?

The usual sequence of events will be as follows: The clerk (who is often the board stenographer) will introduce you to the chairman of the oral board, who will introduce you to the other members of the board. Acknowledge the introductions before you sit down. Do not be surprised if you find a microphone facing you or a stenotypist sitting by. Oral interviews are usually recorded in the event of an appeal or other review.

Usually the chairman of the board will open the interview by reviewing the highlights of your education and work experience from your application – primarily for the benefit of the other members of the board, as well as to get the material into the record. Do not interrupt or comment unless there is an error or significant misinterpretation; if that is the case, do not hesitate. But do not quibble about insignificant matters. Also, he will usually ask you some question about your education, experience or your present job – partly to get you to start talking and to establish the interviewing "rapport." He may start the actual questioning, or turn it over to one of the other members. Frequently, each member undertakes the questioning on a particular area, one in which he is perhaps most competent, so you can expect each member to participate in the examination. Because time is limited, you may also expect some rather abrupt switches in the direction the questioning takes, so do not be upset by it. Normally, a board member will not pursue a single line of questioning unless he discovers a particular strength or weakness.

After each member has participated, the chairman will usually ask whether any member has any further questions, then will ask you if you have anything you wish to add. Unless you are expecting this question, it may floor you. Worse, it may start you off on an extended, extemporaneous speech. The board is not usually seeking more information. The question is principally to offer you a last opportunity to present further qualifications or to indicate that you have nothing to add. So, if you feel that a significant qualification or characteristic has been overlooked, it is proper to point it out in a sentence or so. Do not compliment the board on the thoroughness of their examination – they have been sketchy, and you know it. If you wish, merely say, "No thank you, I have nothing further to add." This is a point where you can "talk yourself out" of a good impression or fail to present an important bit of information. Remember, *you close the interview yourself*.

The chairman will then say, "That is all, Mr. _____, thank you." Do not be startled; the interview is over, and quicker than you think. Thank him, gather your belongings and take your leave. Save your sigh of relief for the other side of the door.

How to put your best foot forward

Throughout this entire process, you may feel that the board individually and collectively is trying to pierce your defenses, seek out your hidden weaknesses and embarrass and confuse you. Actually, this is not true. They are obliged to make an appraisal of your qualifications for the job you are seeking, and they want to see you in your best light. Remember, they must interview all candidates and a non-cooperative candidate may become a failure in spite of their best efforts to bring out his qualifications. Here are 15 suggestions that will help you:

1) Be natural – Keep your attitude confident, not cocky

If you are not confident that you can do the job, do not expect the board to be. Do not apologize for your weaknesses, try to bring out your strong points. The board is interested in a positive, not negative, presentation. Cockiness will antagonize any board member and make him wonder if you are covering up a weakness by a false show of strength.

2) Get comfortable, but don't lounge or sprawl

Sit erectly but not stiffly. A careless posture may lead the board to conclude that you are careless in other things, or at least that you are not impressed by the importance of the occasion. Either conclusion is natural, even if incorrect. Do not fuss with your clothing, a pencil or an ashtray. Your hands may occasionally be useful to emphasize a point; do not let them become a point of distraction.

3) Do not wisecrack or make small talk

This is a serious situation, and your attitude should show that you consider it as such. Further, the time of the board is limited – they do not want to waste it, and neither should you.

4) Do not exaggerate your experience or abilities
In the first place, from information in the application or other interviews and sources, the board may know more about you than you think. Secondly, you probably will not get away with it. An experienced board is rather adept at spotting such a situation, so do not take the chance.

5) If you know a board member, do not make a point of it, yet do not hide it
Certainly you are not fooling him, and probably not the other members of the board. Do not try to take advantage of your acquaintanceship – it will probably do you little good.

6) Do not dominate the interview
Let the board do that. They will give you the clues – do not assume that you have to do all the talking. Realize that the board has a number of questions to ask you, and do not try to take up all the interview time by showing off your extensive knowledge of the answer to the first one.

7) Be attentive
You only have 20 minutes or so, and you should keep your attention at its sharpest throughout. When a member is addressing a problem or question to you, give him your undivided attention. Address your reply principally to him, but do not exclude the other board members.

8) Do not interrupt
A board member may be stating a problem for you to analyze. He will ask you a question when the time comes. Let him state the problem, and wait for the question.

9) Make sure you understand the question
Do not try to answer until you are sure what the question is. If it is not clear, restate it in your own words or ask the board member to clarify it for you. However, do not haggle about minor elements.

10) Reply promptly but not hastily
A common entry on oral board rating sheets is "candidate responded readily," or "candidate hesitated in replies." Respond as promptly and quickly as you can, but do not jump to a hasty, ill-considered answer.

11) Do not be peremptory in your answers
A brief answer is proper – but do not fire your answer back. That is a losing game from your point of view. The board member can probably ask questions much faster than you can answer them.

12) Do not try to create the answer you think the board member wants
He is interested in what kind of mind you have and how it works – not in playing games. Furthermore, he can usually spot this practice and will actually grade you down on it.

13) Do not switch sides in your reply merely to agree with a board member
Frequently, a member will take a contrary position merely to draw you out and to see if you are willing and able to defend your point of view. Do not start a debate, yet do not surrender a good position. If a position is worth taking, it is worth defending.

14) Do not be afraid to admit an error in judgment if you are shown to be wrong

The board knows that you are forced to reply without any opportunity for careful consideration. Your answer may be demonstrably wrong. If so, admit it and get on with the interview.

15) Do not dwell at length on your present job

The opening question may relate to your present assignment. Answer the question but do not go into an extended discussion. You are being examined for a *new* job, not your present one. As a matter of fact, try to phrase ALL your answers in terms of the job for which you are being examined.

Basis of Rating

Probably you will forget most of these "do's" and "don'ts" when you walk into the oral interview room. Even remembering them all will not ensure you a passing grade. Perhaps you did not have the qualifications in the first place. But remembering them will help you to put your best foot forward, without treading on the toes of the board members.

Rumor and popular opinion to the contrary notwithstanding, an oral board wants you to make the best appearance possible. They know you are under pressure – but they also want to see how you respond to it as a guide to what your reaction would be under the pressures of the job you seek. They will be influenced by the degree of poise you display, the personal traits you show and the manner in which you respond.

ABOUT THIS BOOK

This book contains tests divided into Examination Sections. Go through each test, answering every question in the margin. We have also attached a sample answer sheet at the back of the book that can be removed and used. At the end of each test look at the answer key and check your answers. On the ones you got wrong, look at the right answer choice and learn. Do not fill in the answers first. Do not memorize the questions and answers, but understand the answer and principles involved. On your test, the questions will likely be different from the samples. Questions are changed and new ones added. If you understand these past questions you should have success with any changes that arise. Tests may consist of several types of questions. We have additional books on each subject should more study be advisable or necessary for you. Finally, the more you study, the better prepared you will be. This book is intended to be the last thing you study before you walk into the examination room. Prior study of relevant texts is also recommended. NLC publishes some of these in our Fundamental Series. Knowledge and good sense are important factors in passing your exam. Good luck also helps. So now study this Passbook, absorb the material contained within and take that knowledge into the examination. Then do your best to pass that exam.

EXAMINATION SECTION

EXAMINATION SECTION
TEST 1

DIRECTIONS: Each question or incomplete statement is followed by several suggested answers or completions. Select the one that BEST answers the question or completes the statement. *PRINT THE LETTER OF THE CORRECT ANSWER IN THE SPACE AT THE RIGHT.*

1. For a worker to give a client advice based upon what the worker would do in a like situation is generally

    A. *good* practice, principally because it forms a very realistic and human basis for advice
    B. *good* practice, principally because it provides the wisest counsel the worker can give generating from his sympathetic understanding
    C. *poor* practice, principally because it leads the worker into a relationship with the client on a personal level rather than on the more desirable impersonal, professional level
    D. *poor* practice, principally because the client's point of view and motivation may be different from the worker's

1.____

2. For a worker to reassure a client by stating, *"Everything is going to be all right,"* when the worker is aware that everything cannot possibly be all right and that practical help with the client's problem will not be forthcoming for a long time would generally be a

    A. *good* idea, since a client should be shielded as much as possible, for the duration of the crisis period, from the negative factors in a situation
    B. *good* idea, since the worker should be using a supporting relationship to carry out his role as a helping person
    C. *poor* idea, since it does not portray reality and may result in resentment on the part of the client
    D. *poor* idea, since it will develop a feeling of dependence on the part of the client, thus impairing a basic tool of the professional worker

2.____

3. For a worker to finish a sentence for a client who appears to be groping for words when the worker believes he knows what the client wishes to say would generally be

    A. *advisable,* because it facilitates efficient interviewing and aids the client in verbalizing
    B. *advisable,* because it tends to reduce client embarrassment and develop good rapport and mutual understanding between client and worker
    C. *inadvisable,* because it tends to undermine the client's self-reliance and ability to think independently
    D. *inadvisable,* because the client may have wished to say something else and may be too embarrassed or fearful of displeasing to point this out

3.____

4. When interviewing an applicant who is resistive to the extent that the information he gives in answer to the investigator's questions is incomplete and obscure, a worker should FIRST

    A. attempt to understand the character of the applicant and uncover the reasons for his attitude

4.____

B. ignore the applicant's attitude and get whatever information she can from him
C. inform the applicant that concealing relevant facts concerning his case is a basis for prosecution for perjury
D. request the applicant to leave and to return when he is in a better frame of mind

5. After analyzing the information obtained about a client, the worker tells him, "*The reason why you keep quitting jobs is that you think maybe you won't do a good job and will be fired.*"
For the worker to tell this to a client would generally be

   A. *advisable,* as long as the analysis is well-conceived and based upon a sufficient amount of reliable information
   B. *advisable,* if the statement is prefaced by, "On the basis of the information I have, I am convinced that...." since any such analysis is subject to the possibility of error
   C. *inadvisable,* since for greatest usefulness the client should be brought by the discussion to the point where he himself arrives at the explanation for his conduct
   D. *inadvisable,* since the focus of the worker's attention and worker-client relationships should be on effects, not on causes

6. Contact with a client over a period of time involves the worker in a relationship which can lead either to an expression by the client of a direct positive feeling of being accepted or understood, or to an indirect negative response such as breaking subsequent appointments, refusal to talk, etc.
When faced with such a negative response from a client, the worker should realize that

   A. he has failed to use a professional approach to the client
   B. negative, as well as positive, responses are to be expected from most clients
   C. the client is out of touch with reality
   D. there is no significance to such a response and should, therefore, be ignored by the worker

7. The practice of casework in a social agency or institution involves working with a number of clients with a range of problems which confront them in varying life situations.
To say that all cases are psycho-social in nature means that

   A. agency function is the sole determinant of the caseworker's focus
   B. all cases encompass both objective reality and the meaning of reality to the client experiencing it
   C. all casework practice is a form of psychotherapy
   D. equal weighting must be given to psychological and social factors in every case

8. Diagnosis in casework is a process whereby the caseworker strives to determine the underlying causes and contributing factors to the client's social maladjustment.
It is important to have such diagnosis PRIMARILY because

   A. the client may not feel his problems are properly understood unless he is involved in the diagnostic process
   B. unless the underlying causes are treated by the caseworker the client cannot be effectively helped
   C. the diagnostic process may reveal serious psychological pathology that requires treatment by a psychiatrist
   D. it enables the caseworker to establish casework goals that the client can realistically reach

9. When a recipient of public assistance is offered a job which will not pay enough to allow him to get off the relief rolls, he may consider several factors.
Of the following, the factor to which a client who is a marginal worker, frequently out of work and frequently receiving either partial or full public assistance, is likely to give most consideration in deciding whether to attempt to evade taking the job is

   A. his increased status in the community when it is known that he is partially self-supporting
   B. his moral obligation to be self-supporting
   C. whether all his increased expenses will be allowed for when his new budget is determined
   D. whether the work will provide him with satisfaction

10. In professional casework, the individual is helped to take appropriate responsibility for the solution of his own problems. The personal and social adjustment of the individual and its implications for society are stressed. This implies that the professional caseworker

    A. discourages the client from accepting help in order to protect him from feelings of dependency
    B. emphasizes to the client the need for conforming to social standards
    C. recognizes that he has to take over for the client in the solution of his problems as long as he comes to the agency
    D. uses social and psychological methods and techniques based on an assessment of a client's needs and strengths in order to effect change

11. When the worker is aware that her client is grappling with a problem, trying to solve it in a way which social workers would generally consider to be ill-advised, it would usually be BEST for the worker to

    A. maintain an understanding and accepting attitude without involving himself in finding a solution to the problem
    B. point out to the client the most desirable solution to the problem and persuade her to employ this solution
    C. point out to the client the most desirable solution to the problem, but make no effort at persuasion
    D. point out to the client the various alternative solutions to the problem and the implications of each

12. Some time ago, it was proposed that families receiving public assistance might make satisfactory foster parents.
The current status of this proposal is that the plan

    A. has been tried out but did not prove successful largely because the foster parents felt little incentive to continue the burdens of foster parenthood
    B. is now being tried out and is so far working out despite the fact that there is no material incentive to the families to being foster parents
    C. is now being tried out, its prospects for success aided by the fact that the allowances for the foster child are larger than the normal public assistance allowance
    D. is still receiving serious consideration and is expected to be tried out once certain legal and psychological problems have been overcome

13. The Department of Welfare makes a distinction between an abandoned child and a foundling. Both the abandoned child and the foundling have been deserted by his parent or parents, but the abandoned child is

    A. born in wedlock, while a foundling is born out-of-wedlock
    B. deserted after the age of two years, while a foundling is deserted shortly after birth
    C. of unknown identity, while a foundling is left with a note or some other identification
    D. one about whose parents something is known, while a foundling's parents are of unknown identity

14. An applicant for public assistance comes to the intake section of a welfare center. His only assets consist of $36 weekly from unemployment insurance benefits and $54 monthly from a veteran disability allowance.
    For the social investigator to include both sources of income in determining the applicant's need for public assistance would usually be

    A. *correct*, because both unemployment insurance benefits and veteran disability allowances are considered as income in estimating an applicant's needs
    B. *correct*, because only in cases of totally disabled veterans are veteran disability allowances not considered as income in estimating an applicant's needs
    C. *incorrect*, because unemployment insurance benefits are based on former taxed earnings of the applicant and are, therefore, not considered as income in estimating the applicant's needs
    D. *incorrect*, because veteran disability allowances are outright federal grants and are, therefore, not considered as income in estimating an applicant's needs

15. A payment of both principal and interest is due on money owed to a finance company by a client receiving supplementary assistance who has no available resource to meet this debt.
    The one of the following circumstances which is MOST likely to motivate the Department of Welfare to make an allowance to pay this debt is that

    A. a television set and various similar household furnishings may be repossessed
    B. garnishee action is threatened which might result in loss of employment
    C. the debt was contracted before the client was accepted for public assistance, and the Credit Clearance Unit has determined that the interest rate is not higher than the prevailing rate
    D. the debt was contracted during the period when the client was receiving public assistance

16. A recipient of Old Age Assistance notifies his social investigator that he expects to leave town for a two-months' visit with his daughter in Vermont.
    For the social investigator to tell the client that he will lose assistance during the period would be

    A. *correct*; recipients of public assistance must be discouraged from taking costly trips except in cases of visits to extremely ill, very close relatives
    B. *correct*; the recipient may lose all rights to receive assistance if he leaves the state for a period exceeding one month

C. *incorrect*; the recipient may continue to receive assistance if temporarily absent from his legal residence (for a period up to six months) if he cannot meet his needs and is otherwise eligible
D. *incorrect*; the recipient will receive assistance from the State of Vermont during that period, under a mutual assistance law between the two states

17. The one of the following which MOST accurately describes the usual manner in which the city, state, and federal governments meets the costs of the Home Relief program is that

    A. the city and the state share the cost, while the federal government makes no contribution
    B. the city pays the whole cost with no reimbursement from the state or federal government
    C. the city, state, and federal governments share the cost
    D. the state and federal government share the cost, reimbursing the city for its initial outlay

18. The Secretary of Health, Education and Welfare has, within the past several years, issued a series of administrative decisions, one of which relates to income earned by children who are recipients of public assistance.
    Of the following, the MOST significant change in this respect is that income earned by children may be disregarded in computing the family welfare budget if it is

    A. earned through part-time employment of a child under 16 years of age
    B. set aside towards the child's future needs such as education and preparation for employment
    C. used for any purpose of the child or his family which is not deemed to be frivolous or otherwise undesirable
    D. utilized for current uses such as school expenses, extra clothing, and transportation needed for employment

19. *"The practice of casework cannot be learned by intellectual processes alone. Some of the most conspicuous failures each year are persons who have acquired a knowledge of human mechanisms but who, because of a faulty emotional setup, are either unable to relate this knowledge to an understanding of people in trouble or --- worse still --- because of their own needs, use their knowledge sadistically and to the harm of the client."*
    According to the above paragraph, it would be LEAST correct to state with regard to skill in the field of social work that

    A. a faulty emotional set-up may result in a worker's failure to relate his knowledge to an understanding of people in trouble
    B. among the most unsuccessful social workers are some who have been educated to know and understand people and what causes them to function as they do
    C. by using intellectual processes alone, one cannot learn the practice of casework
    D. emotionally motivated, rather than intellectually gifted, people cannot in the long run be successful social caseworkers

20. Employee A is asked a question by Employee B concerning a matter which is B's responsibility primarily. Although A is not certain of the correct answer, he gives one to the best of his knowledge, not indicating his uncertainty. A's action was

   A. *acceptable*; B has the primary responsibility in this matter and is probably only seeking A's informal opinion
   B. *acceptable*; the desire for complete certainty before making a decision leads to useless delay
   C. *not acceptable*; A should have refused to answer B's question since the matter is B's responsibility primarily
   D. *not acceptable*; B may take action on the basis of the uncertain knowledge provided by A

21. A social worker who has problems centered around his acceptance of authority is MOST likely to find it difficult to

   A. relate to people
   B. adhere to agency policies
   C. develop self-awareness in handling clients
   D. cooperate with other services in helping the client

22. In the supervision of young, inexperienced investigators, the MOST important training task for the supervisor is to

   A. encourage investigators to make their own decisions about case problems
   B. give experience-based answers to various problems that arise in cases
   C. teach investigators how to analyze and assess important facts in order to make decisions about case problems
   D. teach investigators how to recognize evidence of mental breakdown

23. In order to be BEST able to teach a newly appointed employee who must learn to do a type of work which is unfamiliar to him, his supervisor should realize that during this first stage in the learning process, the subordinate is generally characterized by

   A. acute consciousness of self
   B. acute consciousness of subject matter, with little interest in persons or personalities
   C. inertness or passive acceptance of assigned role
   D. understanding of problems without understanding of the means of solving them

24. The MOST accurate of the following principles of education and learning for a supervisor to keep in mind when planning a training program for the assistant supervisors under her supervision is that

   A. assistant supervisors, like all other individuals, vary in the rate at which they learn new material and in the degree to which they can retain what they do learn
   B. experienced assistant supervisors who have the same basic college education and agency experience will be able to learn new material at approximately the same rate of speed
   C. the speed with which assistant supervisors can learn new material after the age of forty is half as rapid as at ages twenty to thirty
   D. with regard to any specific task, it is easier and takes less time to break an experienced assistant supervisor of old, unsatisfactory work habits than it is to teach him new, acceptable ones

25. Assume that you are a case supervisor and that you are planning to train a group of experienced social investigators in certain specific skills which they need in their daily work.
The one of the following methods which may generally be expected to be MOST valuable in ascertaining the effectiveness of the training program is to

   A. administer an objective examination to these investigators prior to conducting the training program and an equivalent form of the examination after the program and compare the results
   B. evaluate and compare the work records of these investigators with regard to these skills prior to and after completion of the training program
   C. hold a staff meeting with the investigators after the training program is completed and allow them to discuss frankly their opinions of the values they derived from the various parts of the training
   D. prepare an objective and detailed questionnaire covering the program, have the investigators answer without identifying themselves, and analyze the answers given

25.____

26. A supervisor has received orders for a work assignment to be carried out by his unit. He has firmly decided on methods for carrying out this assignment which he believes will lead to its completion both properly and expeditiously. He has no intention whatsoever of changing his mind. After he has reached his decision, he calls a staff conference to discuss various alternative methods of carrying out the assignments without making clear that he has already decided upon the method to be used.
To hold a conference of this type would generally be a

   A. *good* idea, because his subordinates are likely to carry the assignment through better if they believe that they devised the methods used
   B. *good* idea, because the staff will have the opportunity and be properly motivated to gain knowledge and experience in methodology without endangering staff performance
   C. *poor* idea, because it would be a failure on the part of the supervisor to show the firm leadership which his unit has a right to expect
   D. *poor* idea, because the discovery by the staff that they had not actually participated in deciding upon methods to be used would have an adverse effect upon their morale

26.____

27. Supervisors are frequently faced with the necessity of training old employees in new tasks. An employee inexperienced in a task is much more likely to make a mistake than one who is experienced in it.
In delegating authority to an old employee to perform a new task, a supervisor should generally

   A. delegate the authority as soon as the subordinate gains minimum competence, allowing him to make mistakes which will not do major damage to the client or to the agency program
   B. delegate the authority as soon as the subordinate gains minimum competence, but supervise him closely, enough so that he will not have the opportunity to make even minor mistakes
   C. make the delegation of authority dependent upon the importance which the client places upon the problems involved

27.____

D. grant the authority until the employee has become experienced in performing the task

28. A supervisor has been transferred from supervision of one group of units to another group of units in the same center. She spends the first three weeks in her new assignment in getting acquainted with her new subordinates, their caseload problems, and their work. In this process, she notices that some of the case records and forms which are submitted to her by two of the assistant supervisors are carelessly or improperly prepared.
The BEST of the following actions for the supervisor to take in this situation is to

    A. carefully check the work submitted by these assistant supervisors during an additional three weeks before taking any more positive action
    B. confer with these offending workers and show each one where her work needs improvement and how to go about achieving it
    C. institute an in-service training program specifically designed to solve such a problem and instruct the entire subordinate staff in proper work methods
    D. make a note of these errors for documentary use in preparing the annual service rating reports and advise the workers involved to prepare their work more carefully

29. A supervisor, who was promoted to this position a year ago, has supervised a certain assistant supervisor for this one year. The work of the assistant supervisor has been very poor because he has done a minimum of work, refused to take sufficient responsibility, been difficult to handle, and required very close supervision. Apparently due to the increasing insistence by his supervisor that he improve the caliber of his work, the assistant supervisor tenders his resignation, stating that the demands of the job are too much for him. The opinion of the previous supervisor, who had supervised this assistant supervisor for two years, agrees substantially with that of the new supervisor. Under such circumstances, the BEST of the following actions the supervisor can take, in general, is to

    A. recommend that the resignation be accepted and that he be rehired should he later apply when he feels able to do the job
    B. recommend that the resignation be accepted and that he not be rehired should he later so apply
    C. refuse to accept the resignation but try to persuade the assistant supervisor to accept psychiatric help
    D. refuse to accept the resignation, promising the assistant supervisor that he will be less closely supervised in the future since he is now so experienced

30. After completing a conference with a case supervisor concerning the ramifications of a complex family problem, a social investigator informs the case supervisor that she feels that her assistant supervisor is too strict in her handling of all the social investigators under her supervision, especially in comparison with the other assistant supervisors in the center.
The one of the following actions which is generally BEST for the case supervisor to take is to

    A. advise the investigator in a friendly fashion to apply for a transfer to a unit which has a more lenient supervisor
    B. caution the investigator that complaining about a fellow employee behind her back is frowned upon by higher authority as it is a sign of disloyalty

C. inform the investigator that she, the case supervisor, will investigate the complaint to determine whether or not it has any validity
D. tell the investigator that the closer and stricter a supervisor is, the better and more completely trained will be her subordinate staff

31. Rumors have arisen to the effect that one of the social investigators under your supervision has been attending classes at a local university during afternoon hours when he is supposed to be making field visits.
The BEST of the following ways for you to approach this problem is to

    A. disregard the rumors since, like most rumors, they probably have no actual foundation in fact
    B. have a discreet investigation made in order to determine the actual facts prior to taking any other action
    C. inform the investigator that you know what he has been doing and that such behavior is an overt dereliction of duty and is punishable by dismissal
    D. review the investigator's work record, spot check his cases, and take no further action unless the quality of his work is below average for the unit

32. A supervisor must consider many factors in evaluating a worker whom he has supervised for a considerable time. In evaluating the capacity of such a worker to use independent judgment, the one of the following to which the supervisor should generally give MOST consideration is the worker's

    A. capacity to establish good relationships with people (clients, colleagues)
    B. educational background
    C. emotional stability
    D. the quality and judgment shown by the investigator in previous work situations known to the supervisor

33. A supervisor is conducting a special meeting with the assistant supervisors under her supervision to read and discuss some major complex changes in the rules and procedures. She notices that one of the assistant supervisors who is normally attentive at meetings seems to be paying no attention to what is being said. The supervisor stops reading the rules and asks the assistant supervisor a couple of questions about the changed procedure, to which she gets satisfactory answers.
The BEST action of the following for the supervisor to take at the meeting is to

    A. advise the assistant supervisor gently but firmly that these changes are complex and that her undivided attention is required in order to fully comprehend them
    B. avoid further embarrassment to the assistant supervisor by asking the group as a whole to pay more attention to what is being read
    C. discontinue the questioning and resume reading the procedure
    D. politely request the assistant supervisor to stop giving those present the impression that she is uninterested in what goes on about her

34. A supervisor becomes aware that one of her very competent experienced workers never takes notes during an interview with a client, except to note an occasional name, address, or date. When asked about this practice by the supervisor, the worker states that she has a good memory for important details and has always been able to satisfactorily record an interview after the client has left.
It would generally be BEST for the supervisor to handle this situation by

A. discussing with her that more extensive note-taking may sometimes be desirable with a client who believes note-taking to be evidence that his problem will receive serious consideration
B. agreeing with this practice since note-taking interferes with the establishment of a proper worker-client relationship
C. explaining that since interviewing is an art form rather than an exact science, a good worker must devise her own personal rules for interviewing and not be bound by general principles
D. warning the worker that memory is too uncertain a, thing to be relied upon and, therefore, notes should be taken during an interview of all matters

35. When an experienced subordinate who has the authority and information necessary to make a decision on a certain difficult matter brings the matter to his supervisor without having made the decision, it would generally be BEST for the supervisor to

A. agree to make the decision for the subordinate after the subordinate has explained why he finds it difficult to make the decision and after he has made a recommendation
B. make the decision for the subordinate, explaining to him the reasons for arriving at the decision
C. refuse to make the decision, but discuss the various alternatives with the subordinate in order to clarify the issues involved
D. refuse to make the decision, explaining to the subordinate that he is deemed to be fully qualified and competent to make the decision

36. The one of the following instances when it is MOST important for an upper level supervisor to follow the chain of command is when he is

A. communicating decisions
B. communicating information
C. receiving suggestions
D. seeking information

37. Experts in the field of personnel relations feel that it is generally a bad practice for subordinate employees to become aware of pending or contemplated changes in policy or organizational set-up via the *grapevine* CHIEFLY because

A. evidence that one or more responsible officials have proved untrustworthy will undermine confidence in the agency
B. the information disseminated by this method is seldom entirely accurate and generally spreads needless unrest among the subordinate staff
C. the subordinate staff may conclude that the administration feels the staff cannot be trusted with the true information
D. the subordinate staff may conclude that the administration lacks the courage to make an unpopular announcement through official channels

38. In order to maintain a proper relationship with a worker who is assigned to staff rather than line functions, a line supervisor should

A. accept all recommendations of the staff worker
B. include the staff worker in the conferences called by the supervisor for his subordinates
C. keep the staff worker informed of developments in the area of his staff assignment
D. require that the staff worker's recommendations be communicated to the supervisor through the supervisor's own superior

39. Of the following, the GREATEST disadvantage of placing a worker in a staff position under the direct supervision of the supervisor whom he advises is the possibility that the

    A. staff worker will tend to be insubordinate because of a feeling of superiority over the supervisor
    B. staff worker will tend to give advice of the type which the supervisor wants to hear or finds acceptable
    C. supervisor will tend to be mistrustful of the advice of a worker of subordinate rank
    D. supervisor will tend to derive little benefit from the advice because to supervise properly, he should know at least as much as his subordinate

40. One factor which might be given consideration in deciding upon the optimum span of control of a supervisor over his immediate subordinates is the position of the supervisor in the hierarchy of the organization. It is generally considered proper that the number of subordinates immediately supervised by a higher, upper echelon, supervisor

    A. is unrelated to and tends to form no pattern with the number supervised by lower level supervisors
    B. should be about the same as the number supervised by a lower level supervisor
    C. should be larger than the number supervised by a lower level supervisor
    D. should be smaller than the number supervised by a lower level supervisor

41. An important administrative problem is how precisely to define the limits on authority that is delegated to subordinate supervisors.
    Such definition of limits of authority should be

    A. as precise as possible and practicable in all areas
    B. as precise as possible and practicable in areas of function, but should allow considerable flexibility in the area of personnel management
    C. as precise as possible and practicable in the area of personnel management, but should allow considerable flexibility in the areas of function
    D. in general terms so as to allow considerable flexibility both in the areas of function and in the areas of personnel management

42. The LEAST important of the following reasons why a particular activity should be assigned to a unit which performs activities dissimilar to it is that

    A. close coordination is needed between the particular activity and other activities performed by the unit
    B. it will enhance the reputation and prestige of the unit supervisor
    C. the unit makes frequent use of the results of this particular activity
    D. the unit supervisor has a sound knowledge and understanding of the particular activity

43. A supervisor is put in charge of a special unit. She is exceptionally well-qualified for this assignment by her training and experience. One of her very close personal friends has been working for some time as a social investigator in this unit. Both the supervisor and investigator are certain that the rest of the investigators in the unit, many of whom have been in the bureau for a long time, know of this close relationship.
    Under these circumstances, the MOST advisable action for the supervisor to take is to

A. ask that either she be allowed to return to her old assignment or, if that cannot be arranged, that her friend be transferred to another unit in the center
B. avoid any overt sign of favoritism by acting impartially and with greater reserve when dealing with this investigator than with the rest of the staff
C. discontinue any socializing with this investigator either inside or outside the office so as to eliminate any gossip or dissatisfaction
D. not to review the situation with the investigator in order to arrive at a mutually acceptable plan of proper office decorum

44. In a conference on difficult cases between a recently appointed assistant supervisor and an experienced, above-average social investigator, the MOST valuable of the following services that the assistant supervisor can offer the investigator is a

    A. detached point of view
    B. knowledge of human needs
    C. knowledge of the agency's basic rules and regulations
    D. willingness to make decisions

45. Much attention has been focused of late in social welfare circles on ways of reaching and helping multi-problem families.
    The one of the following approaches which is MOST important as an early step in working with these families is

    A. contacts with educational, social, vocational, and religious services in the community to see what resources there might be for referral
    B. referral to appropriate resources for medical or psychiatric care
    C. the worker's taking active responsibility for determining its needs with the family and for helping them secure all of the needed discretionary services for which they are legally eligible
    D. thorough determination of the causative factors responsible for the difficulties facing the family and the extent to which each member of the family has been responsible therefor

46. In helping young investigators in their work with aged clients, one of the MOST important, and often MOST difficult, principles to get across is the need

    A. for knowledge of various community services for the aged, i.e., different kinds of placement facilities, recreational resources, etc.
    B. to move more slowly with old people, e.g., to repeat explanations, etc.
    C. to recognize that old people are different from each other and need to be individualized just as other clients do
    D. to take more responsibility for planning with aged clients

47. The MOST important of the following reasons why the average resident of a deteriorated slum neighborhood resists relocation to an area in the suburbs with better physical accommodations is that he

    A. does not recognize as undesirable the characteristics which are responsible for deterioration of the neighborhood
    B. has some expectation of neighborly assistance in his old home in times of stress and adversity
    C. hopes for better days when he may be able to become a figure of some importance and envy in the old neighborhood

D. is attuned to the noise of the city and fears the quiet of the suburbs

48. From a psychological and sociological point of view, the MOST important of the following dangers to the persons living in an economically depressed area in which the only step taken by governmental and private social agencies to assist these persons in the granting of a dole is that

    A. industry will be reluctant to expand its operations in that area
    B. the dole will encourage additional non-producers to enter the area
    C. the residents of the area will probably have to find their own solution to their problems
    D. their permanent dependency will be fostered

49. The term *real wages* is generally used by economists to mean the

    A. amount of take-home pay left after taxes, social security, and other such deductions have been made by the employer
    B. average wage actually earned during a calendar or fiscal year
    C. family income expressed on a per capita basis
    D. wages expressed in terms of its buying power

50. Most authorities in the field of special education believe that the BEST of the following actions to take in connection with the education of a blind child of pre-school age is to

    A. arrange to have the blind child educated in a home or nursery school setting with one sighted child on whom he can depend for help with his needs
    B. enroll the blind child in a nursery school with sighted children when he is ready for group experience
    C. have the blind child taught simple games and handicrafts at home in a sheltered setting apart from the pressure of group activity and competition with sighted children
    D. place the blind child in a residential school for the totally blind where he can become more comfortable and adjusted to his condition in the company of his blind peers

51. It has at times been suggested that an effective way to eradicate juvenile delinquency would be to arrest and punish the parents for the criminal actions of their delinquent children.
    The one of the following which is the CHIEF defect of this proposal is that

    A. it fails to get at the cause of the delinquent act and tends to further weaken disturbed parent-child relationships
    B. since the criminally inclined child has apparently demonstrated little love or affection for his parents, the child will be unlikely to amend his behavior in order to avoid hurting his parents
    C. the child who commits anti-social acts does so in most cases in order to hurt his parents so that this proposal would not only increase the parents' sorrow but would also serve as an incentive to more delinquency by the child
    D. the punishment should be limited to the person who commits the illegal action rather than to those who are most interested in his welfare

52. Surveys which have compared the relative stability of marriages between white persons with marriages between non-white persons in this country have shown that among blacks there is

    A. a significantly higher percentage of spouses absent from the household than among whites
    B. a significantly higher percentage of spouses absent from the household than among whites living in the South, but the opposite is true in the Northeast
    C. a significantly lower percentage of spouses absent from the household than among whites
    D. no significant difference in the percentages of spouses absent from the household when compared with the white population

53. A phenomenon found in the cultural and recreational patterns of European immigrant families in America is that, generally, the foreign-born adults

    A. as well as their children, tend to retain and continue their old-world activities and adopt the cultural and recreational customs of America
    B. as well as their children, tend to retain and continue their old-world cultural and recreational pursuits, finding it equally difficult to adopt those of America
    C. tend soon to drop their old pursuits and adopt the cultural and recreational patterns of America while their children find it somewhat more difficult to make this change
    D. tend to retain and continue their old-world cultural and recreational pursuits while their children tend to rapidly replace these by the games and cultural patterns of America

54. Certain mores of migrant groups are strengthened under the impact of their contact with the native society while other mores are weakened. In the case of Puerto Ricans who have come to New York City, the effect of such contact upon their traditional family structure has been a _____ of the former _____ family structure.

    A. *strengthening; maternalistic*
    B. *strengthening; paternalistic*
    C. *weakening; maternalistic*
    D. *weakening; paternalistic*

55. Administrative reviews and special studies by independent experts, as reported by the present Secretary of Health, Education and Welfare, indicate that the proportion of recipients of public assistance who receive such assistance through willful misrepresentation of the facts is

    A. less than 1%
    B. about 4%
    C. between 4% and 7%
    D. between 7% and 10%

Questions 56-60.

DIRECTIONS: Answer Questions 56 through 60 SOLELY on the basis of the following three charts concerning referrals made by the Department of Welfare of the City of Millville.

TABLE 1. REFERRALS MADE FOR SPECIALIZED HELP

	Number of Referrals For			
Year	Psychiatric Help	Alcoholism	Vocational Rehabilitation	Homemaking Service
2003	110	60	180	20
2004	120	36	205	36
2005	80	25	275	40
2006	90	16	250	40
2007	100	5	230	38

TABLE 2. RESULTS OF REFERRALS FOR VOCATIONAL REHABILITATION

Year	Total Referrals	Appeared For Initial Interviews	Kept Appointments, Cooperative	Treatment Successful	Off Welfare As Result Of Treatment
2003	180	120	40	30	25
2004	205	180	120	80	60
2005	275	220	160	120	100
2006	250	215	160	130	105
2007	230	220	170	128	90

TABLE 3.
Average Percentage of "Budget for Specialized Help" Expended on Each Category for the five-year period 2003-07.

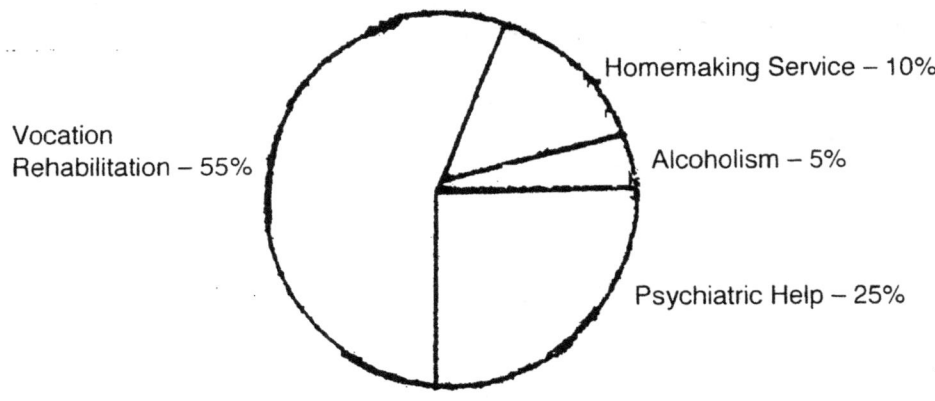

56. Of the following, the two years when an equal percentage of clients who were cooperative when referred for vocational rehabilitation were successfully treated were

   A. 2003 and 2004
   B. 2003 and 2005
   C. 2004 and 2006
   D. 2005 and 2006
   E. 2006 and 2007

57. If, in 2006, the number of referrals had been increased for alcoholism by 10, for vocational rehabilitation by 40, and for homemaking services by 5, then the total number of referrals for specialized help that year would have increased by MOST NEARLY

   A. 1.5%   B. 7%   C. 14%   D. 30%   E. 55%

58. Although there are actually no errors in the charts given above, suppose that one of the following figures was recorded incorrectly and constituted the one and only error in the charts.
   By carefully inspecting the charts, one could always tell that there was an error if the error was made in the figure for the

   A. average percentage utilization for psychiatric help of the "Budget for Specialized Help" from 2003 through 2007
   B. number of referrals for alcoholism in 2007
   C. number of referrals for vocational rehabilitation who were removed from welfare as a result of treatment in 2005
   D. number referred for vocational rehabilitation in 2006 who appeared for initial interview

59. In 2005, the budget for specialized help was $200,000, and the amount expended for vocational rehabilitation was $8,000 more than the amount represented by the average percentage expended for vocational rehabilitation for the period 2003 through 2007.
   The amount expended for vocational rehabilitation in 2005 was MOST NEARLY

   A. $4,400   B. $19,000   C. $44,000   D. $110,000   E. $118,000

60. Assume that the average size of the budget for specialized help for the five-year period 2003 through 2007 was $360,000 per year.
   The average cost per referral for psychiatric help during this period was MOST NEARLY

   A. $180   B. $360   C. $720   D. $900
   E. cannot be determined from the data given

KEY (CORRECT ANSWERS)

1. D	16. C	31. B	46. C
2. C	17. A	32. D	47. B
3. D	18. B	33. C	48. D
4. A	19. D	34. A	49. D
5. C	20. D	35. C	50. B
6. B	21. B	36. A	51. A
7. B	22. C	37. B	52. A
8. D	23. A	38. C	53. D
9. C	24. A	39. B	54. D
10. D	25. B	40. D	55. A
11. D	26. D	41. A	56. B
12. C	27. A	42. B	57. C
13. D	28. B	43. A	58. D
14. A	29. B	44. A	59. E
15. B	30. C	45. C	60. D

EXAMINATION SECTION
TEST 1

DIRECTIONS: Each question or incomplete statement is followed by several suggested answers or completions. Select the one that BEST answers the question or completes the statement. *PRINT THE LETTER OF THE CORRECT ANSWER IN THE SPACE AT THE RIGHT.*

1. Recently, the State Department of Labor declared that *city employers are faced with a developing manpower shortage which will grow worse if business continues at high levels.* Since public welfare agencies have a special responsibility for preserving the self-maintenance capacities of physically handicapped persons, it is appropriate that during periods of increased employment such as that illustrated above, the Department of Welfare should place its GREATEST emphasis on

    A. developing special placement opportunities for all disabled persons
    B. providing vocational training for newly opened job opportunities
    C. recognizing that the disabled can never become as self-maintaining as the physically fit and will, therefore, continue to need assistance
    D. directing the disabled to those occupations related to the special senses which the disabled often develop
    E. facilitating the efforts of the disabled to obtain employment, whether temporary or permanent, partial or total

1.____

2. In order to meet more adequately the public assistance needs occasioned by sudden changes in the national economy, welfare agencies in general recommend, as a matter of preference, that

    A. each locality build up reserve funds to care for needy unemployed persons in order to avoid a breakdown of local resources such as occurred during the Depression
    B. the federal government assume total responsibility for the administration of public assistance
    C. state settlement laws be strictly enforced so that unemployed workers will be encouraged to move from the emergency industry centers to their former homes
    D. a federal-state-local program of general assistance be established with need as the only eligibility requirement
    E. eligibility requirements be tightened to assure that only legitimately worthy local residents receive the available assistance

2.____

3. The MOST practical method of maintaining income for the majority of aged persons who are no longer able to work, or for the families of those workers who are deceased, is

    A. a comprehensive system of non-categorical assistance on a basis of cash payments
    B. an integrated system of public assistance and extensive work relief programs
    C. a coordinated system of providing care in institutions and foster homes
    D. a system of contributory insurance in which a cash benefit is paid as a matter of right
    E. an expanded system of diagnostic and treatment centers

3.____

4. With the establishment of insurance and assistance programs under the Social Security Act, many institutional programs for the aged have tended to the greatest extent toward an increased emphasis on providing, of the following types of assistance,

    A. care for the aged by denominational groups
    B. care for children requiring institutional treatment
    C. recreational facilities for the able-bodied aged
    D. training facilities in industrial homework for the aged
    E. care for the chronically ill and infirm aged

5. According to studies made by the Federal Security Agency, the benefits received by beneficiaries of the old age and survivors insurance program during past years

    A. were too small to be basically helpful
    B. represented about a third of the resources of most beneficiaries
    C. were an unimportant factor in income maintenance
    D. constituted the major portion of the family's income
    E. constituted about one-quarter of the average public assistance grant

6. Of the following terms, the one which BEST describes the Social Security Act is

    A. enabling legislation   B. regulatory statute
    C. appropriations act   D. act of mandamus
    E. provisional enactment

7. Of the following, the term which MOST accurately describes an *appropriation* is

    A. authority to spend   B. itemized estimate
    C. *fund* accounting   D. anticipated expenditure
    E. executive budget

8. When business expansion causes a demand for labor, the worker group which benefits MOST immediately is the group comprising

    A. employed workers
    B. inexperienced workers under 21 years of age
    C. experienced workers 21 to 25 years of age
    D. inexperienced older workers
    E. experienced workers over 40 years of age

9. The MOST important failure in our present system of providing social work services in local communities is the

    A. absence of adequate facilities for treating mental illness
    B. lack of coordination of available data and service in the community
    C. poor quality of the casework services provided by the public agencies
    D. limitations of the probation and parole services
    E. inadequacy of private family welfare services

10. It is generally considered advisable for a public assistance agency to make special allowances for the purchase of physical appliances for its recipients only when the

    A. desired appliance has been prescribed by a physician and when the client is physically, mentally, and emotionally able to use it
    B. agency has a special fund to meet such additional expenditures

C. fact is verified that employment will be available if the client uses the appliance
D. purchase will assure the individual of becoming self-maintaining again
E. desired appliance has been prescribed by a social worker as necessary to compensate the client for loss of a normal bodily function

11. Recent studies of the relationship between incidence of illness and the use of available treatment services among various population groups in the United States show that

    A. while lower-income families use medical services with greater frequency, total expenditures are greater among the upper-income group
    B. although the average duration of a period of medical care increases with increasing income, the average frequency of obtaining care decreases with increasing income
    C. adequacy of medical service is inversely related to frequency of illness and size of family income
    D. families in the higher-income brackets have a heavier incidence of illness and make greater use of medical service than do those in the lower-income brackets
    E. both as to frequency and duration, the distribution of illness falls equally on all groups, but the use of medical service increases with income

11.____

12. The category of disease which most public health departments and authorities usually are NOT equipped to handle directly is that of

    A. chronic disease
    B. bronchial disturbances
    C. venereal disease
    D. mosquito-borne diseases
    E. incipient forms of tuberculosis

12.____

13. Recent statistical analyses of the causes of death in the United States indicate that medical science has now reached the stage where it would be preferable to increase its research toward control, among the following, PRINCIPALLY of

    A. accidents   B. suicides
    C. communicable diseases   D. chronic disease
    E. infant mortality

13.____

14. Although the distinction between mental disease and mental deficiency is fairly definite, both these conditions USUALLY represent

    A. diseases of one part or organ of the body rather than of the whole person
    B. an inadequacy existing from birth or shortly afterwards, and appearing as a simplicity of intelligence
    C. a deficiency developing later in life and characterized by distortions of attitude and belief
    D. inadequacies in meeting life situations and in conducting one's affairs
    E. somewhat transitory conditions characterized by disturbances of consciousness

14.____

15. According to studies made by reliable medical research organizations in the United States, differences among the states in proportion of physicians to population are MOST directly related to the

    A. geographic resources among the states
    B. skill of the physicians

15.____

C. relative proportions of urban and rural people in the population of the states
D. number of specialists in the ranks of the physicians
E. health status of the people in the various states

16. MOST of the mentally ill who are hospitalized for long periods of time are in institutions administered by

   A. the U.S. Public Health Service
   B. county and municipal government
   C. the Veterans Administration
   D. the state government
   E. psychiatrists in private practice

17. In the development and maintenance of a social group work program, it is accepted that certain principles must be recognized if the program is to achieve maximum value.
Of the following, the one consideration which would be INAPPROPRIATE as a base on which to set the planning and operation of such a program is that it should

   A. be individualized and designed to meet specific needs
   B. develop out of interests and needs of group members
   C. be planned, conducted, and evaluated by the group
   D. involve the group worker as a helping person
   E. develop from a series of initial and follow-up surveys conducted by trained personnel

18. One of the MAIN advantages of incorporating a charitable organization is that

   A. gifts or property of a corporation cannot be held in perpetuity
   B. gifts to unincorporated charitable organizations are not deductible from the taxable income
   C. incorporation gives less legal standing or *personality* than an informal partnership
   D. members of a corporation cannot be held liable for debts contracted by the organization
   E. a corporate organization cannot be sued

19. In conjunction with court and educational authorities, the Division of Physically Handicapped Children administers a program of care for persons under 2-1 years of age who, by reason of physical defect or infirmity, are totally or partially incapacitated for education or occupation. All of the following types of care are provided by this division EXCEPT

   A. surgical treatment
   B. medical treatment
   C. therapeutic treatment
   D. furnishing of prosthetic appliances or devices
   E. procuring scholarships for summer camps

20. If a client is to receive continuing services or assistance from the Department of Welfare requests help in which the Department has an interest and which it cannot provide, but which can be furnished by another agency in the community, the worker should USUALLY

A. interpret the other agency's function to the client and determine how best to use its services, thus conserving the client's time and preventing possible embarrassment to him
B. forego discussion of the other agency's services with the client, since it is confusing for two welfare agencies to attempt to serve the same client at the same time
C. send a case summary to the other agency and request that a worker from that agency call at the client's home to assist in the working out of his problem
D. not suggest the agency to which the client can apply and ask him to return and discuss the plans developed with the other agency
E. not advise the client that his situation will be discussed with another agency in the community and that he will be notified whether the agency can accept his case and be of service to him

21. It is important to use a skilled worker to conduct the initial interview with an applicant for assistance in the Department of Welfare CHIEFLY because

    A. inaccurate information concerning eligibility requirements and the documentary evidence which must be produced may then be checked expeditiously
    B. whenever possible, the assistance plan should be developed during the course of the first interview
    C. only a highly skilled worker can make a satisfactory investigation of the applicant's eligibility
    D. the relationship established between worker and applicant during this interview usually determines the departmental policies affecting the case
    E. the effectiveness of the Department's subsequent work with the client is often influenced materially by the kind of relationship established in this first contact

22. During an interview, a client may seem overwhelmed by the amount of data needed by the Department of Welfare in order to establish his eligibility, although most of the required information, as a rule, is easily obtained.
The one of the following responses by the intake interviewer which could be expected to reassure such a client BEST is

    A. "All this information is very important and you should try your best to get it as soon as possible"
    B. "If you think you'll have trouble getting this material together, I'll do it for you"
    C. "It sounds like a lot, but it is actually very simple; without realizing it, you probably have most of the material on hand already"
    D. "There's no need to be overwhelmed by the amount of this material; all our clients have to get it together"
    E. "Oh, I'm sure you can do it"

23. Of the following objectives, the one which an initial interview with an applicant for public assistance is usually designed to serve is to

    A. afford the client an opportunity to express his needs and desires
    B. allow the worker time to secure all the information he wants
    C. condition the direction of service
    D. record verbatim the client's statement regarding need
    E. include a discussion of the client's family and other personal relationships

24. A MOST appropriate condition in the use of direct questions to obtain personal data in an interview is that, whenever possible,

   A. the direct questions be used only as a means of encouraging the person interviewed to talk about himself
   B. provision be made for recording the information
   C. the direct questions be used only after all other methods have failed
   D. the person being interviewed understand the reason for requesting the information
   E. the direct questions be used only at the start of the interview

25. Suppose that a social investigator, during his initial interview with a client, notices that the client is becoming antagonistic for no apparent reason.
In this situation, the investigator should USUALLY

   A. explain to the client that unwarranted antagonism is really due to factors deeply hidden in the client's own personality
   B. terminate the interview with a statement to the effect that the client should return for another interview when he feels more kindly disposed toward the interviewer
   C. make clear in his actions that there is no retaliatory disapproval and continue to try to understand the client's difficulties
   D. admit to the client that he is aware of the existing antagonism and that he is unable to find the reason for it
   E. ask the client why he feels antagonistic toward him since he himself has not given him any grounds for such a reaction

26. When a client informs the social investigator of a plan to move permanently to another state, it is the responsibility of the investigator to advise the client that

   A. he should apply for continued approval of his grant on the basis of *temporary absence* since his plan for permanent removal may not materialize
   B. the last check he receives before leaving the city should be used for necessary transportation and expenses while traveling to his new abode
   C. he will be ineligible for any continued assistance from the Department of Welfare and that eligibility in the new community will depend upon local requirements
   D. he should not move to a new state since the assistance in that state will probably not be adequate for his needs
   E. the Department of Welfare will arrange to have the public assistance agency in the community to which he is going make an immediate investigation in order that the continuance of his public assistance grant will not be interrupted

27. Suppose that the mother of a family receiving public assistance is recovering from an operation at home and that her doctor reports she will be unable to care for her children for one month.
In such a situation, it would be MOST appropriate for the social investigator to

   A. recommend the assignment of a Department of Welfare homemaker in accordance with the doctor's report
   B. refer the children to a temporary shelter
   C. visit the neighborhood to find a free home for the children
   D. recommend that foster care be provided
   E. write to legally responsible relatives living in an adjacent state to explore the possibility of their providing care for the children

28. In computing the budget for a family applying for public assistance where there is a lodger living in the household, Department of Welfare policy requires that the social investigator should deduct the

   A. total income received from the lodger from the total estimate of the family's needs
   B. total income from the lodger minus the cost of food for any meals provided from the total estimate of the family's needs
   C. total income from the lodger minus an adjusted allowance for fuel and lighting
   D. net income from the total estimate of the family's needs
   E. total income received from the lodger minus the proportionate cost of room rental

29. Experiences with respect to use of cash payments to public assistance clients have established that, basically, this form of assistance is more satisfactory than any other type because cash payments

   A. are less destructive of the client's self-respect than relief in kind
   B. are less likely to call for bookkeeping skill than payments by requisition
   C. are cheaper to administer than other forms of assistance
   D. are more acceptable to commercial concerns than order slips
   E. make possible larger grants to clients than other forms of assistance

Questions 30-39.

DIRECTIONS: Levels of approval for certain types of allowances are set forth in the Department of Welfare manual, POLICIES GOVERNING THE ADMINISTRATION OF PUBLIC ASSISTANCE. In Questions 30 through 39 below are listed certain types of allowances for which approval is necessary according to departmental policy. Answer each of these questions in the following manner:

ANSWER   IF THE TYPE OF ALLOWANCE REQUIRES APPROVAL OF
A. - the unit supervisor only
B. - the case supervisor in addition to the unit supervisor
C. - case consultation, in addition to unit and case supervisors
D. - case consultation and the resource division, in addition to unit and case supervisors
E. - the resource division, in addition to unit and case supervisors

30. Bond and mortgage waiver, after refusal to execute.

31. Carfare to attend a special school for the blind and deaf.

32. Conditional sale and mortgage on personal property.

33. Emergency assistance, first recurring or non-recurring agent.

34. Repair allowance for a homeowner.

35. Housing project security deposit.

36. Guide fees for blind persons.

37. Rent arrears, including costs and fees.

38. Special diet, upon medical recommendation. 38.____

39. Referral of a homeless man to a municipal shelter. 39.____

40. Coordination of staff activity in a large agency can usually be effected MOST successfully by an executive through the use of 40.____

   A. written reports
   B. face-to-face contact in meetings with department heads
   C. observation of performance
   D. permanent assignment of staff to specific functions
   E. procedural instructions

41. Organization charts and manuals are essential to the sound administration of a public welfare agency. 41.____
   In this respect, the MOST important purpose of a manual in the Department of Welfare is to serve as a

   A. means of preventing duplication
   B. device for eliminating community misinterpretation of the Department's activities
   C. tool for achieving orderly operations
   D. method of maintaining executive controls
   E. system of compiling case decisions

42. Failure on the part of a caseworker in a public assistance agency to recognize the close relationship between standards of performance with regard to office routine and standards of work with clients is, of the following, usually due to the fact that 42.____

   A. his supervisor has continued to assume responsibilities which the case worker should carry
   B. his supervisor has not made clear to the case worker each aspect of the job or of the total responsibilities of the worker
   C. the case worker should not be the person who is required to prepare reports
   D. the case worker's primary function is the treatment of social problems
   E. the clerical staff has not adequately performed those of its duties related to the work of the case worker

43. In helping a social investigator deal with a case in which the client is harassed by a difficult family situation, the supervisor usually can be of GREATEST assistance by 43.____

   A. showing the investigator that his own family experiences parallel those of the client
   B. helping the investigator balance the interests of all members of the family
   C. advising the investigator that family matters are frequently too personal to be discussed in detail
   D. suggesting that a psychiatrist be brought in on the case
   E. teaching the investigator how to discover which member of the family is most maladjusted

44. Initial interviews with applicants for public assistance require a high degree of skill on the part of the interviewer PRIMARILY because

    A. applicants are usually uncertain as to what kind of factual information will aid their cause
    B. applicants who have had no previous experience with social agencies usually are overwhelmed by the newness of the experience
    C. the feeling of economic dependency is usually emotionally disturbing to the applicant
    D. applicants are naturally suspicious of any agency that administers public funds
    E. the worker and the applicant are strangers to one another and each is uncertain as to how the other will interpret his remarks

45. During a case conference, if a unit supervisor repeatedly returns to a statement of points already made, the case supervisor should USUALLY

    A. discuss some neutral subject until the unit supervisor is more composed
    B. insert a question leading to a different topic altogether
    C. terminate the conference as soon as possible in order not to waste time
    D. attempt to direct the flow of discussion by expressing his own opinion on the subject
    E. let the unit supervisor talk himself out on this topic

46. With respect to case recording, the Department of Welfare has developed a new type of streamlined case record which will contain all the essential factors pertinent to current eligibility and which can be maintained in a usable and readable condition on a continuing basis. The development of this plan was based on a consideration of the essential attributes of good recording in a public assistance agency. Of the following, the one which is NOT in accord with the above-mentioned plan is

    A. accuracy in recording, which reflects the point of view of the client and of the social investigator
    B. elimination of all information except the documentation of eligibility based on points of statutory evidence
    C. freedom from bias or prejudice in order that the client may receive the full service due to him
    D. brevity and conciseness, which make the record more serviceable for review by the social investigator and by his supervisors
    E. clarity, which is obtained largely by adherence to common rules of rhetoric and which provides coherence and unity

47. When Children's Placement Services refers an undercare case to a welfare center for public assistance, the social investigator to whom the case is assigned should

    A. review the investigation made by Children's Placement Services and supplement it with whatever information is necessary
    B. accept the case as referred for the appropriate type of public assistance
    C. make a complete investigation of all factors of eligibility in the same manner as for any other applicant for public assistance
    D. talk to the client and make a referral to a private agency
    E. make an immediate referral of the client to an available job in order to prevent dependency

48. Under certain circumstances, a court order imposes responsibility on the unmarried mother and the father for sharing the support of a child born out of wedlock. The court which has jurisdiction over such matters is the

    A. Supreme Court
    B. Children's Court
    C. Magistrates' Court
    D. Domestic Relations Court
    E. Court of Special Sessions

49. Social workers who work principally with maladjusted children find that the children's problems MOST frequently originate in

    A. health factors
    B. religious attitudes
    C. teachers' attitudes
    D. parental attitudes
    E. economic conditions

50. Persistent feeding difficulties in children are MOST often related to

    A. poverty in the home
    B. basic personality maladjustments
    C. high intelligence
    D. the presence of other children in the room
    E. the number of older and younger children in the family

51. If a person attempts to conceal his inadequacies in certain activities by overindulging in some other activity, he is MOST liable to do so because he

    A. is compensating for his inadequacies
    B. has a delusion that he is inadequate in some activities
    C. has rationalized that the skill in the latter activity is more easily developed
    D. is trying to develop skill in the former activities by indulging in the latter
    E. is projecting the pleasure he finds in the former activities to the latter

52. The casework concept of *acceptable,* when applied to behavior that deviates from what society expects, implies

    A. refusing to pass judgment on the behavior of others
    B. accepting all behavior without attempting to evaluate it
    C. condoning behavior which the client seems incapable of changing
    D. exercising non-judgmental impartiality
    E. active understanding of the underlying feelings rather than of the behavior itself

53. When a prospective employer requests that a person of a particular race, color, or religion be sent to him in order to fill a job opening in a department store, the employment interviewer should IMMEDIATELY

    A. report the employer to the State Commission Against Discrimination
    B. advise the employer that he is violating the law and that if he does not accept an able and available person, he will be reported to the State Commission Against Discrimination
    C. remove the employer's name as a source of employment referrals and notify Central Office so that other welfare centers may be informed of the situation
    D. arrange to interview the employer in order to determine whether there are valid reasons for his request
    E. make an employment referral if a public assistance recipient who meets the specifications of the employer is available

54. The early English Poor Laws influenced American administration of relief in their emphasis upon the

   A. giving of adequate assistance
   B. centralization of relief administration under a national authority
   C. local character of administration and financing
   D. failure to enforce the responsibility of relatives for their needy kin
   E. discrimination made in providing for the care and treatment of clients on the basis of their individual needs

55. The undifferentiated treatment of clients given by public welfare services in the eighteenth and nineteenth centuries was due not only to the state of social and economic development but also to the

   A. limitations imposed by the lack of adequate institutional facilities
   B. prevalence of religious condemnation of social inadequacy
   C. absence of technical knowledge necessary for social diagnosis
   D. homogeneous nature of the social structure itself
   E. relative isolation of individual communities

KEY (CORRECT ANSWERS)

1. E	16. D	31. A	46. B
2. D	17. E	32. C	47. A
3. D	18. D	33. A	48. E
4. E	19. E	34. E	49. D
5. D	20. A	35. A	50. B
6. A	21. E	36. B	51. A
7. A	22. C	37. B	52. D
8. B	23. A	38. A	53. B
9. B	24. D	39. A	54. C
10. A	25. C	40. B	55. C
11. C	26. C	41. C	
12. A	27. A	42. B	
13. D	28. A	43. B	
14. D	29. A	44. C	
15. C	30. D	45. B	

EXAMINATION SECTION
TEST 1

DIRECTIONS: Each question or incomplete statement is followed by several suggested answers or completions. Select the one that BEST answers the question or completes the statement. *PRINT THE LETTER OF THE CORRECT ANSWER IN THE SPACE AT THE RIGHT.*

1. Because of public reaction incident to an announcement of revised public assistance allowances, the members of your staff express concern over how to justify the position of the department.
   As a supervisor, you should inform your staff that the revised allowances represent a _____ allowance to meet essential needs.

   A. new policy based on furnishing a minimum
   B. new policy based on furnishing a minimum but adequate
   C. continuing policy based on furnishing a minimum
   D. continuing policy based on furnishing a minimum but adequate

   1.____

2. Good public relations are essential to the sucess of a public welfare agency's program. Of the following means of maintaining good public relations, the MOST important for the public welfare agency is

   A. the development of a cooperative, interested attitude on the part of the *press*
   B. the education of the community as a whole by the regular release of informative but lively human interest stories
   C. concern for the welfare of the clients and prompt and efficient methods of meeting need
   D. the development of good relationships with the other social agencies in the community to insure their support of the agency's program

   2.____

3. Although human relations have large significance in the job of the supervisor in the Department of Welfare, it is NOT necessarily true that the

   A. supervisor must be a leader in order to do his job well
   B. supervisor must be able to tell his staff how to do their jobs in the right way
   C. supervisor is part of the management of the Department of Welfare
   D. ability to get along with people is the sole stock in trade of the supervisor

   3.____

4. Management is the art and science of preparing, organizing, and directing human effort applied to control the forces and utilize the materials of nature for the benefit of man. From the point of view of an employee in the Department of Welfare, this statement means that when he is promoted to the position of supervisor,

   A. he will be working directly with the raw materials of the social service field in dealing with clients
   B. he will no longer be concerned so much with *human relations* as when he dealt with clients directly in the capacity of social investigator
   C. his efforts from then on should be directed toward doing things himself
   D. his efforts from then on should be directed toward getting others to do things

   4.____

5. Office organization charts, if they are to be used as aids to proper supervision of Welfare Department personnel, should be

   A. used as originally drawn up so that the type of organization function can be easily memorized by the entire staff
   B. revised constantly because office organizations are constantly undergoing change
   C. eliminated entirely and developed in some new form since no organization chart is an accurate representation of actual working conditions
   D. checked against actual working conditions in order to present a current and accurate state of affairs

6. A sustained relationship between supervisor and subordinate staff is necessary because the

   A. department must avoid needless expenditure of public funds
   B. worker learns to relate himself helpfully to clients as he learns to take help from the supervisor
   C. worker must have some source from which to get answers to his problems
   D. case problems in public assistance require a degree of skill that social investigators do not have themselves

7. Looking at the job of the supervisor in the Department of Welfare in terms of production or accomplishment, one may BEST say that, of the following, the *tools* with which the supervisor does his work are

   A. rules and regulations
   B. records and orders
   C. office equipment
   D. people

8. The supervisor carries out his responsibility for maintaining the department's standards of case work practice by

   A. delegating responsibility for the case load to the assistant supervisors and social investigators and reviewing and passing on their work in each case
   B. delegating responsibility for the case load to the assistant supervisors and social investigators and directing their activities in relation to each case
   C. establishing and using controls necessary to keep aware of case load activity and interviewing where there is indication of breakdown in the standards of practice
   D. individual development through supervisory conferences and training meetings

9. A supervisor is transferred to a new district office. In a group conference with his staff on the first day, he should

   A. discuss with them their ways of relating to the previous supervisor and tell them that, for the present, he will fit into the established schedule
   B. tell them about himself, his ways of working, what he expects of his staff, and the methods of supervision he intends to follow
   C. learn as much as possible about each member of the staff so that he can get down to a constructive relationship with them as soon as possible
   D. conduct only a brief introductory meeting in a friendly manner without reference to the work situation

10. It is the conception of the Department of Welfare that the plan to distribute checks semi-monthly to families approved for public assistance

    A. represents an entirely new experiment in the methods of distributing relief allowances
    B. is required by law since relief allowances must be received in advance
    C. will make management easier for relief recipients
    D. must be adopted even against its better judgment because of recommendations made by the Federal Security Agency

11. The degree of success or failure which can be achieved with applications of the official service rating system now in use depends MAINLY on the

    A. immediate supervisor of the employee being rated
    B. the Municipal Civil Service Commission
    C. the employee being rated
    D. the central office of the Department of Welfare

12. The step-by-step process of training a subordinate by instruction, regardless of what is to be taught, is

    A. preparation of the learner, presentation of instruction matter, performance tryout, follow-up
    B. presentation of instruction matter, performance try-out, preparation of learner, follow-up
    C. performance tryout, follow-up, preparation of the learner, presentation of instruction matter
    D. presentation of instruction matter, performance tryout, follow-up

13. Supervisors in the Department of Welfare should caution staff personnel to avoid over-willingness to do things for the client because

    A. they are not charged with any responsibility toward the client
    B. all possible resources must be exhausted before anyone may become a recipient of public assistance
    C. this approach to the client may foster dependency
    D. eligibility is established by the written record, and the personal factor does not enter into it

14. A unit supervisor on your staff reports that one of the recipients of public assistance in his case load is a war veteran who held National Service Life Insurance during the Gulf War for a period of ten months, but who has done nothing to collect his share of the dividend.
    You should advise this unit head that

    A. the veteran cannot receive any dividend since he held the insurance less than one year
    B. the veteran should apply for the dividend since any funds received as a result of such payments must be budgeted as a resource
    C. the veteran should apply for the dividend since these funds are legally exempt from any use except in the manner to be determined by the recipient
    D. whether the veteran wishes to apply for the dividend is subject to his own wishes and not within the purview of the Department of Welfare

15. A CORRECT evaluation by the supervisor of the conference method as compared with parliamentary procedure would be that the group conference

    A. inhibits the expression of free opinion
    B. dispenses with the technicalities of formal debate
    C. is slow and awkward when considered in terms of requirements of the work of the Department of Welfare
    D. makes for easier control of the situation by the person in charge of the meeting

16. Faced with the alternative of conducting a conference or giving a lecture to a group of associates in the Department of Welfare, your decision in favor of the lecture would be justified only if

    A. your mental equipment is superior to that of the group
    B. you wish to make sure that every member of the group gains something from the meeting
    C. the time element is of some importance
    D. the subject to be considered is beyond the experience and knowledge of the group

17. The group conference as distinguished from the individual conference as a method of staff development can be used BEST when

    A. the material to be covered is informational
    B. it might be difficult to handle individual reactions to the material of the meeting
    C. there is a training need that is more or less common to the group
    D. the group is not too divergent in background and level of development

18. Good supervision is selective because

    A. it is not necessary to direct all the activities of the person
    B. a supervisor would never have time to know the whole case load of a worker
    C. workers resent too much help from a supervisor
    D. too much case reading is a waste of valuable time

19. In developing the supervisory relationship with an assistant supervisor, a supervisor should aim to

    A. give the assistant supervisor a feeling of strength on which he can depend for case decisions
    B. give the assistant supervisor a feeling of security so that he can be flexible in his application of policy and procedure when necessary
    C. be as cooperative as possible so that the assistant supervisor will be cooperative with his staff in return
    D. be as interested as possible in the assistant supervisor's personal problems which he feels are affecting his work

20. At the end of his probationary period, a supervisor should be considered potentially valuable in his position if he shows

    A. awareness of his areas of strength and weakness, identification with the administration of the department, and ability to learn under supervision
    B. skill in case work, supervision, and administration, and a friendly, democratic approach to the staff

C. knowledge of departmental policies and procedures and ability to carry them out, ability to use authority, and ability to direct the work of the staff
D. an identification with the department, acceptance of responsibility, and ability to give help to the individuals who are to be supervised

21. Suppose that during the first two months of your assignment as supervisor in the Department of Welfare, you receive numerous suggestions from the staff for the improvement of working conditions, production, etc.
You should

    A. inform the administrator that the large number of suggestions submitted must be evidence that something is seriously amiss in the management of the office
    B. ignore the suggestions for the time being since you are not sufficiently acquainted with your new assignment
    C. inform the staff that, in due time, every suggestion will receive your attention and such action as the facts may warrant
    D. call a brief meeting and explain that it would be inadvisable for you to take any action until you have at least completed your probationary period

22. After two months in a district office, you have an assistant supervisor who rarely comes to you for help, presents no cases for discussion at conferences, and discusses no problems of administration or personnel in his unit. He is friendly toward you in manner and accepts any suggestions you make, but seeks nothing from you.
As supervisor, you should

    A. select a random sampling of cases from his unit for review, review his unit controls, show him everything is not as fine as he imagined, and point out where he needs help
    B. discuss his transfer to another office with your administrator since there is apparently a personality clash between you
    C. continue the relationship as currently established, using every opportunity that presents itself to waken his interest in learning, to challenge his capacities, and to show him where you may have something to offer him
    D. draw up an evaluation in which you outline his strengths and weaknesses, and discuss this with him, particularly his failure to utilize supervision

23. Occasional participation of assistant supervisors and social investigators on committees formulating new procedures would be in line with good supervisory practice because

    A. they are the only ones who know from experience how present procedures are working out
    B. they thereby acquire an understanding of the difficulties to be overcome in getting agreement in the central office
    C. assistant supervisors and social investigators throughout the department will have a greater tendency to accept changes if their own groups have participated in the preliminary thinking
    D. all the assistant supervisors and social investigators will be better prepared to accept the changes because the committee members shared developments with them

24. In planning for the vacation period of an assistant supervisor, the BEST course of action for the supervisor to follow is to

   A. take responsibility for supervision of the unit himself as this will give him an opportunity to get to know the staff, to renew his skills in supervision of workers, and to evaluate the assistant supervisor from the knowledge of the unit so gained
   B. let the more responsible and capable workers take turns at the desk for one day each week to give them an opportunity to supervise and to show them that the supervisor is democratic in his relations with the staff
   C. leave the unit uncovered because workers should be able to function independently for a few weeks as long as the unit clerk can keep administrative controls going
   D. arrange for two other supervisors to divide the work of the unit and add to their normal responsibilities the supervision of staff and management of the unit for the period

25. An assistant supervisor complains to you about one of his workers who turns every conference into a battle by arguing every point made.
As supervisor, you should

   A. help the supervisor work out techniques of conference direction that will avoid his presentation of an opinion against which the worker can argue
   B. help the supervisor relate this behavior to the total knowledge about the worker to see whether a personality difficulty is involved
   C. arrange for a transfer of either worker or supervisor because obviously the latter is too new to handle such a difficult situation
   D. tell him to threaten to charge the worker with insubordination if he does not desist and come to conference in a more receptive mood for learning

26. An assistant supervisor has been in your office about a month. In her relations with staff, management of the unit, and conference with you, she seems to be making at least average adjustment and progress. In your group meetings, however, she contributes nothing to the discussion, raises no questions, takes occasional notes.
As supervisor, you should

   A. call on her for opinion or comment several times at each meeting until she gets accustomed to talking
   B. discuss her conduct directly with her at conference, finding out the source of the difficulty and working out an adjustment
   C. review her personnel folder to see if it throws a light on the problem and direct the content of the next group conference to an aspect of the job in which you know she is particularly interested
   D. recognize that some people are naturally reticent in large groups, and if her contribution in general to the unit is good, do not become concerned about this at all

27. The intake supervisor in the district in which you are supervisor tells you that he has never been able to manage a scheduled, limited conference relationship because of the nature of his job. When he needs help on a case, it must be available immediately because the client is right in the office, and he never can be regular in attendance at a scheduled conference because his workers need him to be available to them at all times.
In this situation, you should

A. tell him that you cannot work in this hit-or-miss fashion, and he will have to conform as do the other supervisors
B. accept his explanation because it is a busy office and there are tremendous pressures in intake
C. excuse the intake supervisor from future conferences
D. tell him you will schedule future conferences with him to begin directly after his arrival and before starting on the day's routine activities

28. As supervisor, you are assigned a recently promoted assistant supervisor who has had five years of experience as an investigator but no professional training or other social work experience.
In your first regular conference with him, you should

    A. give him an opportunity to discuss how his previous experience will help him in this new assignment and how he thinks you can be of help to him
    B. share with him some of your thinking and philosophy about supervision and agency function and let him discuss his thinking with you so that you get to know each other and form the basis for a relationship
    C. make this conference a typical conference and begin immediately to consider the problems he has met in his first days in the unit
    D. ask him what use he wants to make of the supervisory conference and adapt the content and method to suit his wishes

29. An assistant supervisor comes to conference periods regularly and seems ready to discuss any cases or problems you, as supervisor, present, but in the two months you have been supervising him, he has never brought any cases for discussion or raised any problems. When asked, he always says everything in his unit is *fine*.
Of the following, the LEAST constructive approach would be to

    A. put it to him very directly that he was not making good use of supervision and that you expect him to participate equally with you in this process
    B. review how your relationship with him got started and how it has developed in order to understand the problem better
    C. discuss one aspect of his unit functioning in detail to see what he meant by *fine* and how well he understood the problem
    D. bring nothing to the next few conferences yourself so that the burden of the discussion will be thrown on him

30. While attending a unit conference as an observer at the invitation of another supervisor, you hear an assistant supervisor emphasize the value of thorough knowledge of procedures raised by his staff without looking up a single point in the manual.
Asked by the supervisor what you should do about such an assistant supervisor in one of your units, you should reply that

    A. such a situation would not occur in any of your units because your staff has been trained differently
    B. you would discuss methods of staff development at your next individual conference with such an assistant
    C. you would do nothing about this because the statement made by the assistant supervisor may be entirely correct
    D. you cannot answer because this problem affects his unit and not any of yours

31. In developing good methods of recording. the BEST statement of principle to give staff as a guide is to

   A. record everything considered to be pertinent to understanding the needs of the client, his eligibility for assistance, his capacity and efforts in self-help, and the worker's services and relationship with him
   B. follow an outline of record that will tell him what to read and where to place each item
   C. eliminate everything that took place at the interview except those few facts affecting eligibility and need
   D. record everything exactly as it happened so that nothing will be left out that might be useful at some later date

32. Overwhelmed with the feeling of responsibility for nearly one thousand cases, a relatively new assistant supervisor seeks your help in the problem of case reading.
As supervisor, you should

   A. reassure him that it would be neither necessary nor advisable for him to know the entire case load in order to function adequately
   B. tell him that as a new supervisor, he is not expected to know any of the cases
   C. ask him what his plan is and give him help and support in working it out
   D. suggest that he read blocks of cases from one worker at a time so that he will become familiar with each personality and their various methods of working

33. *Hostility toward a supervisor is an unavoidable concomitant of growth.*
In teaching a new group of supervisors, lately promoted from the field, the supervisor sh

   A. point out the fallacy in this idea as being the result of poor supervision rather than any supervision
   B. prepare them to maintain an interest in and a supporting relationship with their workers even where they are showing intensive hostility
   C. recognize the presence of hostility and deal with it immediately so that it does not interfere with the relationship
   D. avoid opportunities for the development of hostility by being as democratic and friendly as possible

34. Of the adjustments that must be made in moving up from assistant supervisor to supervisor, the MOST important at the outset is to

   A. effect a change in the nature of the relationship already developed with the assistant supervisors in the office
   B. get hold of the outstanding reports and unfinished work in the district and complete these
   C. make a statistical analysis of the case load to see what the problems are in general
   D. develop a cooperative relationship with the other supervisors

35. The supervisor's responsibility for maintaining the standard of eligibility in the case load is BEST carried out by

   A. reading as many cases as possible until he has firsthand knowledge of what is being done in the case load

B. delegating this responsibility through the assistant supervisors to the workers and establishing qualitative and quantitative case load controls
C. a good in-service training program
D. teaching the staff in his charge the department's concept of its standard eligibility and helping them individually to approach this standard as the maximum level of their ability

36. In evaluating a new worker at the end of his probationary period, the supervisor should consider the BEST criteria to consist of

   A. knowledge of agency policy and procedure, skill in social study, skill in interviewing, ability to help clients more toward independent solution of problems
   B. identification with the purposes of the agency, interest in people, ability to meet his own needs and to assist others, ability in the learning role and beginnings of skill in social study and diagnosis
   C. identification with the agency, good administrative ability, interest in meeting other people's needs, skill in establishing eligibility, ability to say no to ineligible clients
   D. ability to meet the demands of the case load without too great dependence on supervision, ability to remain objective at all times, skill in case work processes

37. In helping an assistant supervisor select cases for a new worker to carry in his first days with the agency, the MOST important single factor to clarify is that the supervisor must

   A. know the case situation intimately himself
   B. go over the case line-by-line with the worker to be sure the worker has a grasp of the problems presented
   C. select cases that the worker can become readily interested in
   D. select cases that would challenge the worker by the nature of the problem presented

38. Of the following, the MOST appropriate point of view concerning departmental policy and procedure for a supervisor to develop in assistant supervisors is that

   A. they are in the most responsible and strategic spot to influence formulation and revision of policy because they see its effect in practice and have the means of communicating this to the administration
   B. the assistant supervisor must see that the workers carry out policy in every case
   C. they should adapt policy to meet the needs of particular cases not met by any other community resource
   D. they should encourage their workers to provide for the client necessary case action or assistance not covered by departmental policy or procedure

39. Of the following, the MOST important contribution that a supervisor can make to the growth and development of assistant supervisors is to

   A. be available to them whenever they feel a need for consultation
   B. give them definite authority and responsibility for the complete operation of their units, support them in their decisions, and give them help where indicated
   C. have regular conferences with each of them for discussion of problems of unit management or case situations that are too difficult to handle alone
   D. give them a feeling that the supervisor is sharing with them the difficulties of their jobs and is working with them toward a solution of these

40. In reading the case of a worker in her unit, an assistant supervisor finds so many errors in knowledge and judgment and such lack of skill in interviewing that she comes to you for help in dealing with the worker.
As supervisor, you should advise the assistant supervisor to

   A. let the worker discuss the case as he sees it, discovering the problems on his own
   B. go over the case with the worker, showing up each error and discussing it constructively with him
   C. consider the development and degree of security of the worker, selecting those areas for discussion where the worker will be able to recognize the problems and to handle them constructively himself
   D. discuss the problems bearing on eligibility since these are of primary importance in the Department of Welfare

41. An intake supervisor asks your help in deciding whether a certain client is presumptively eligible to receive assistance. This appears to be an unusual case, and the intake supervisor is experiencing a great deal of difficulty in determining how current policy is applicable to the case. After studying all the data submitted for your inspection, you, the supervisor, find that you also do not know what action should be taken.
Under the circumstances, you should

   A. instruct the intake supervisor to ask the client for additional information
   B. advise the intake supervisor to accept the case because the benefit of the doubt should be resolved in favor of the applicant
   C. find out what decisions were made in similar cases
   D. ask Case Consultation for an interpretation of the policy to be applied in this case

42. Because of a consistently high rate of applications for assistance and a very active case load situation, it has been necessary to increase the intake department of a large welfare center to twelve intake interviewers, three appointment interviewers, three receptionists, and six service workers. The administrator and you, the supervisor, are planning to request additional supervisory staff.
Of the following, the MOST feasible action would be to

   A. request an additional assistant supervisor in order to split the responsibilities, having one supervisor over the intake interviewers and the other over the rest of the staff
   B. request the appointment of an assistant supervisor to be responsible for the entire intake department, with two assistant supervisors for direct supervision of the staff
   C. advise Central Office that the Welfare Center is too large and should be split into two
   D. request an additional assistant supervisor and break up the intake section into two departments on a territorial basis, having applicants and clients go to the unit which is responsible for the part of the district in which they live

43. A relatively inexperienced assistant supervisor asks his supervisor to arrange for the reassignment of one of his experienced social investigators because the investigator does not seek or use supervisory help.
The supervisor should respond to this situation by

KEY (CORRECT ANSWERS)

1. D	11. A	21. C	31. A	41. D
2. C	12. A	22. C	32. A	42. B
3. D	13. C	23. C	33. B	43. B
4. D	14. B	24. D	34. A	44. A
5. D	15. B	25. A	35. D	45. A
6. B	16. D	26. C	36. B	46. C
7. D	17. C	27. D	37. A	47. D
8. C	18. A	28. C	38. A	48. C
9. A	19. B	29. A	39. B	49. B
10. C	20. D	30. B	40. C	50. B

EXAMINATION SECTION
TEST 1

DIRECTIONS: Each question or incomplete statement is followed by several suggested answers or completions. Select the one that BEST answers the question or completes the statement. *PRINT THE LETTER OF THE CORRECT ANSWER IN THE SPACE AT THE RIGHT.*

1. Frequent reference has been made to a *safety net* of basic social services by which the needy would be maintained in spite of budget cuts.
   Which of the following pairs of items is NOT included in the term *safety net*?

    A. Social Security and SSI
    B. Unemployment Insurance and Workers' Compensation
    C. Medicaid and Municipal Health Services
    D. Home Relief and AFDC

2. As a supervisor in an office that provides direct services to clients, your case managers and team supervisors are constantly under stress caused by the necessity to make decisions, particularly those which may permanently change clients' lives, as in cases involving adoption, institutionalization, or removal of a child from home.
   Of the following, you can BEST assist staff in reducing these client-related pressures by

    A. providing them with a clear understanding of authority and specific guidelines regarding who is to make decisions under particular circumstances
    B. assuring them that the Agency head has ultimate responsibility for critical decisions affecting clients' lives
    C. helping them understand that clients have the right to self-determination and are largely responsible for making critical decisions
    D. training them to be realistic and objective, thus relieving them of the burden of responsibility for unfavorable client-related decisions

3. Of the following, the MOST important reason why group methods are effective in working with disadvantaged clients is that these clients

    A. are less likely to express feelings of anger in a group setting
    B. may resent discussing any personal problems with individual workers
    C. are more likely to share information about themselves in a group setting
    D. usually seek the approval of others for their actions

4. As a Supervisor II responsible for the operation of three units, you find that one of your units has a particularly high rate of turnover. Clients are complaining that their cases have been mismanaged because of the staff shortage. Of the following, the FIRST action you should take in this situation is to

    A. reassign caseworkers so that all units have coverage
    B. try to determine why workers are unwilling to work in this unit
    C. ask for additional help from your supervisor
    D. handle some of the caseload yourself

5. A new Supervisor I from another Human Resources Administration (HRA) component has been assigned to your office. The LEAST useful way to orient him to the job is to

   A. set up a regular conference schedule to discuss any questions and problems that arise
   B. give him all procedures to read and review them with him
   C. phase in the workload gradually within an agreed upon time frame
   D. ask him to work independently and make independent decisions as much as possible

6. You find that there is an important procedural error in a memo which you distributed to your staff several days ago. The BEST approach for you to take at this time is to

   A. send a corrected memo to the staff, indicating what prior error was made
   B. send a corrected memo to the staff without mentioning the prior error
   C. tell the staff about the error at the next monthly staff meeting
   D. place the corrected memo on the office bulletin board

7. The primary responsibility of a Liaison and Adjustment Unit in an Income Maintenance Center is to assist in resolving clients' appeals of Departmental decisions affecting their eligibility for public assistance.
   In order to ensure that the unit's decisions are in compliance with agency and governmental regulations, it is MOST important for the supervisor of the unit to

   A. review all appeals for Fair Hearings prior to assignment to subordinates
   B. routinely hold staff meetings to discuss the unit's performance
   C. regularly review agency rules and governmental laws regarding public assistance
   D. maintain records in order to insure equalization of the work flow

8. Your supervisor asks you, a Supervisor II, about the status of the response to a letter from a public official concerning a client's case. When you ask the subordinate who was assigned to prepare the response to give you the letter, the subordinate denies that it was given to him. You are certain that the subordinate has the letter, but is withholding it because the response has not yet been prepared.
   Of the following, in order to secure the letter from the subordinate, you should FIRST

   A. accuse the subordinate of lying and demand that the letter be given to you immediately
   B. say that you would consider it a personal favor if the subordinate would find the letter
   C. continue to question the subordinate until he admits to having been given the letter
   D. offer a face-saving solution, such as asking the subordinate to look again for the letter

9. As a Supervisor II, you have been assigned to write a few paragraphs to be included in the agency's annual report, describing the Department of Social Services this year as compared to last year.
   Which of the following elements basic to the agency is LEAST likely to have changed since last year?

   A. Mission   B. Structure   C. Technology   D. Personnel

10. A female client calls you, a Supervisor II, to complain that a male caseworker employed by a vendor agency has requested that she have sexual relations with him in return for the help he has given to her.
    In this situation, you should FIRST tell the client that

    A. you will call the head of the vendor agency and have the caseworker dismissed
    B. she must submit her complaint in writing as soon as possible so that you can investigate the situation
    C. you will immediately call the head of the vendor agency and report her complaint
    D. she must report this complaint to the Office of the Inspector General

11. As a Supervisor II, you have been informed that a grievance has been filed against you, accusing you of assigning a subordinate to out-of-title tasks.
    Of the following, the BEST approach for you to take is to

    A. waive the grievance so that it will proceed to a Step II hearing
    B. immediately change the subordinate's assignment to avoid future problems
    C. respond to the grievance, giving appropriate reasons for the assignment
    D. review the job description to ensure that the subordinate's tasks are not out-of-title

12. Assume you are a Supervisor II in a division that requires supervisory staff from the various units to discuss work related issues. You notice that two of your unit supervisors refuse to talk to each other.
    The BEST action to take in this situation is to

    A. ask one of your other supervisors what he thinks is the cause of the situation
    B. call a staff meeting to explain the importance of harmony among the staff
    C. ignore the situation and hope that in time their relationship will improve
    D. discuss ways to resolve the problem with the two supervisors

13. Assume that you are a Supervisor II who has recently been assigned to a new office. One of your subordinates is performing below standard in several of his assigned tasks. A review of the personnel folder does not indicate any previous problems.
    Of the following, the LEAST appropriate action for you to take is to

    A. hold a series of regularly scheduled conferences with the subordinate to discuss work problems
    B. advise the subordinate to improve his performance or request a transfer
    C. discuss the matter with your supervisor in order to develop a plan for supervision and performance review
    D. bring the matter to the subordinate's attention to develop a mutual understanding of the problem

14. Which of the following is NOT a correct statement about agency group training programs in a public service welfare agency?

    A. Training sessions continue for an indefinite period of time.
    B. Group training sessions are planned for designated personnel.
    C. Training groups are organized formally through administrative planning.
    D. Group training is task-centered and aimed toward accomplishing specific educational goals.

15. As a Supervisor II, you have received an assignment with an instructional sheet regarding a new procedure in Family and Adult Services. You do not quite understand part of the instructions.
    The BEST way to handle this is to

    A. try to carry out the assignment in accordance with your interpretation of the instructions
    B. interpret the assignment according to the previous procedure
    C. explain to your workers that you are not responsible for the instructions
    D. ask your supervisor to clarify the instructions for you

16. You are a Supervisor II responsible for a unit that is required to handle a large number of emergency cases in addition to the regular caseload.
    In order to prevent the continual assignment of emergency cases to the same workers, it is GOOD practice to

    A. assign cases in rotation
    B. redistribute cases to equalize the caseload
    C. designate a daily emergency worker
    D. interpret eligibility requirements more strictly

17. You are a Supervisor II who often holds group meetings with your staff to discuss problem cases.
    This method of supervision is LEAST valuable for

    A. providing an effective way of disseminating information
    B. dealing with individual needs for knowledge and skills
    C. involving staff in unit decision-making
    D. learning from the supervisor and each other

18. A caseworker in a program for which you are responsible advises you that she and her supervisor, a Supervisor I, have a disagreement over what services should be provided in a specific case.
    As the Supervisor II, the FIRST action you should take is to

    A. tell the caseworker to follow the advice of the Supervisor I
    B. meet with both the caseworker and the Supervisor I to hear their arguments
    C. review the case in question to become familiar with the material
    D. tell the caseworker and the supervisor to settle the matter between themselves

19. You are a case supervisor in a General Social Services district office. Your director informs you that a recent audit report indicates that the case managers in your district are making fewer than the required number of field visits per field day. It occurs to you that a substantial number of such visits are probably not being recorded on the Field Activity Reports.
    The FIRST step you should take in this situation is to

    A. review a random sample of Field Activity Reports and case records
    B. write a memorandum to the team supervisor requesting that all field visits be properly documented
    C. call a meeting of all case managers and the team supervisor to discuss the field visit procedure
    D. advise the director that you feel the audit is based on incomplete information

20. A Supervisor I under your direction tells you that he regularly cannot account for one of his caseworker's whereabouts, and his frequent absence causes problems in the assignment of cases and telephone coverage.
In this situation, you should FIRST

   A. tell the supervisor to have the absent worker account for his time
   B. ask the supervisor what action he has taken to have the worker document his time
   C. hold a meeting with the worker and the supervisor to discuss the problem
   D. tell the supervisor to meet with the unit as a whole to discuss the problem

21. You are the Supervisor II in a General Social Services district office. The director of the office has asked you to determine why a particular unit consistently submits its work late. The MOST effective step to take FIRST is to

   A. inform the unit supervisor that he will receive a negative performance evaluation if the situation does not improve
   B. inform the unit supervisor that you have analyzed the situation and expect him to carry out the solution you offer
   C. ask the unit supervisor to assess the situation and take corrective action
   D. meet with the unit supervisor and mutually discuss the problems and what should be done to resolve them

22. As a Supervisor II, you have submitted a memo to your supervisor requesting a conference to discuss the performance of a Supervisor I under your supervision. The memo states that the Supervisor I has a good working relationship with her staff; however, she tends to interpret agency policy too liberally and shows poor administrative skills by missing some deadlines and not keeping proper controls.
Which of the following steps should NOT be taken in order to prepare for this conference with your Supervisor III?

   A. Collect and review all your notes regarding the Supervisor I's prior performance.
   B. Outline your agenda so that you will have sufficient time to discuss the situation.
   C. Tell the Supervisor I that you will be discussing her performance with your supervisor.
   D. Clearly define objectives which will focus on improving the Supervisor I's performance.

23. Assume that you are training and guiding a new supervisor who has spent a number of years as a caseworker and who says that she feels more comfortable with a participatory rather than a directive leadership style, since participation more closely reflects her previous experience.
You should advise her that, of the following, use of the participatory style is LEAST effective when

   A. staff has information which bears on the issue
   B. participants derive ego-satisfaction from the tasks
   C. the supervisor and workers have different goals and interests
   D. tasks are ambiguous and complex

24. You are a Supervisor II assigned to the personnel section of your agency. A friend in one of the divisions, whom you know to be an excellent employee, requests that you recommend to his supervisor or director that he be considered for promotion.
    The BEST course of action for you to take is to

    A. *comply* with his request since he is a friend of yours
    B. *comply* with his request because you know his director is noted for never recommending employees for promotion
    C. *reject* the request and inform the director of the program of your friend's unethical behavior
    D. *reject* the request since only his supervisor or the director of the program can submit such a recommendation

25. As a Supervisor II, you are about to plan an informational meeting with your staff regarding a new reporting form. Which of the following should NOT be included in preparing for this meeting?

    A. Defining the purpose clearly
    B. Preparing a written agenda
    C. Inviting all levels of staff
    D. Allowing time for questions and answers

KEY (CORRECT ANSWERS)

1.	B	11.	C
2.	A	12.	D
3.	C	13.	B
4.	B	14.	A
5.	D	15.	D
6.	A	16.	C/A
7.	C	17.	B
8.	D	18.	C
9.	A	19.	A
10.	C	20.	B

21.	D
22.	C
23.	C
24.	D
25.	C

TEST 2

DIRECTIONS: Each question or incomplete statement is followed by several suggested answers or completions. Select the one that BEST answers the question or completes the statement. *PRINT THE LETTER OF THE CORRECT ANSWER IN THE SPACE AT THE RIGHT.*

1. During a supervisory conference with your unit supervisors, you learn that on the previous day one of the workers in your program gave some confidential case information to an investigative reporter.
   As the Supervisor II, of the following, the FIRST action for you to take in this situation is to

   A. inform the director about the incident
   B. advise the Office of the Inspector General
   C. ask the worker the details of what occurred
   D. assign a new worker to the case

   1.____

2. You have been asked by your director to prepare a memo to the staff describing a new procedure.
   In writing the memo, of the following, the MOST important thing to keep in mind is that the

   A. memo should include all data the staff will need in order to implement the procedure
   B. language of the memo should be as direct as possible
   C. staff should be informed that they are expected to act on the content of the memo
   D. tone of the memo should be polite and encouraging so that the staff will respond favorably

   2.____

3. Mr. Smith, a Supervisor I under your supervision, gives you a memorandum requesting approval to issue emergency clothing funds to one of his clients. After reviewing the request, you find that Mr. Smith has failed to include essential client information in the memorandum. Because of the client's emergency need, of the following, the BEST approach for you to take in this situation is to

   A. approve the request and set aside time to work with Mr. Smith on memo preparation
   B. ask pertinent questions to get the information you need to approve the request
   C. ask Mr. Smith to review the case and to revise the memo to include the additional information
   D. deny the request due to insufficient information

   3.____

4. As a Supervisor II in a General Social Services district office, you have received a telephone call from a neighborhood resident who informs you that she has just witnessed the man next door physically abusing his wife and children and shouting obscenities at them. When assigning the case, of the following, you should advise the Supervisor I and caseworker to

   A. call the police so that they can be at the home when the caseworker arrives
   B. call the wife and give her the address of the battered women's shelter
   C. make an immediate home visit to assess the case and develop a service plan
   D. assist the wife in securing an order of protection for her and the children

   4.____

5. Because of staff shortages, a Supervisor II assigns the unit's best worker to handle occasional difficult cases in addition to the regular caseload. The other workers in the unit are not assigned these difficult cases.
This method of making assignments is

    A. *advisable* because staff shortages must be overcome
    B. *advisable* because this worker will handle the difficult cases better
    C. *inadvisable* because of the *equal work for equal pay* concept
    D. *inadvisable* because the worker will be overburdened

6. As a Supervisor II in a General Social Services district office, you have been requested to develop a resource inventory for your district.
Such an inventory is LEAST valuable in identifying

    A. providers of special services in your district's community
    B. service needs not being met in your district
    C. service definitions to be used by service providers in your district
    D. alternate funding sources to meet special service needs in your district

7. During the weekly conference with your unit supervisors, you tell them that the workers are not completing the new required forms on time, thus delaying provision of services to clients. The supervisors state that the new forms are very complicated and that the workers need training in filling them out.
In order to determine whether training is necessary, as the Supervisor II, of the following, the LEAST appropriate action you should take would be to

    A. revise the form to make it more simple
    B. find out whether the workers know how to complete the form
    C. study the form to see if the instructions are clear
    D. discuss with the supervisors other possible reasons for the workers' poor performance

8. As the field supervisor for a program in Special Services for Children, you have become aware that one of the provisional caseworkers has been arriving late, leaving early, and, on occasion, failing to advise anyone of his whereabouts during working hours.
Since you know that the worker has been effective in handling client problems, the MOST appropriate step for you to take is to

    A. write a report of the situation and submit it to the director
    B. advise the worker that he faces disciplinary action
    C. call the worker in for a conference to discuss the problem
    D. consider possible transfer to another program within the agency

9. A Supervisor I newly assigned to your unit in an Income Maintenance Center has a history of closing cases whenever the eligibility decision is a close one. He boasts about how much money he saves the government with each case closed. However, many of his closed cases have had to be reopened on appeal; and, in several instances, hasty closings have resulted in the breakup of families and the placement of children.
Of the following, the approach MOST likely to modify this supervisor's views would be to

    A. appeal to his humanity so that he will have a greater empathy for his clients
    B. order him to fully document all reasons for future closings

C. meet with his unit and reprimand them for closing eligible cases
D. discuss with him the actual cost to the government, such as the expense of child placement

10. In the course of reviewing case records being sent to you for your approval, you find that many errors are being made in relation to a certain procedure.
The FIRST step for you to take in this situation is to

A. send a memo to staff asking them to review the procedure
B. bring the situation to the attention of the director
C. call your subordinate supervisors together to discuss the problem
D. develop a training program to review the procedure

11. You are a Supervisor II responsible for keeping accurate records of the status of the cases being handled by the units under your supervision.
Of the following, the types of statistical controls which would be LEAST helpful to you are those that

A. help you to spot trouble early
B. analyze every component of your supervisors' tasks
C. enable you to pinpoint cases that are exceptions to the norm
D. provide you with statistical comparisons among units performing the same tasks

12. Assume that you are a Supervisor II in a field office. One of your Supervisor I's tells you that the unit was ordered by the Deputy Director, who is a Supervisor III, to perform a task in a way which is clearly not in accordance with standard procedure.
In this situation, the BEST action for you to take is to

A. discuss the matter with the Supervisor III to learn why the order was given
B. tell the Supervisor I to disregard the order and continue following standard procedure
C. report to the director that the Supervisor III is interfering with your supervision of your unit
D. tell the Supervisor I to obey the order for now but to revert to standard procedure if trouble arises

13. As a Supervisor II in the Office of Staff Development and Training, you supervise five field instructors (Supervisor I's). Two of the five are frequently late in submitting their weekly statistical reports.
The MOST appropriate action for you to take FIRST in this situation is to

A. meet with both supervisors for a three-way discussion of the problem
B. distribute a memo to all staff, stressing the need to complete all reports on time
C. discuss the problem at your next supervisory meeting
D. meet individually with each of the two supervisors involved

14. During the past two months, one of your most competent supervisors has done less effective work and appears listless and preoccupied.
In order to get him back to his former high level of productivity, which of the following steps should you take FIRST?

A. Reassign a substantial portion of his work, to take some of the pressure off him.
B. Work with him to plan his day so he can more effectively use his time.

C. Tell the supervisor you have observed that he appears to be preoccupied lately and ask him what is wrong.
D. Tell the supervisor that he should go on sick leave until he feels better.

Questions 15-18.

DIRECTIONS: Questions 15 through 18 are to be answered SOLELY on the basis of the information contained in the chart below.

PUBLIC ASSISTANCE CASES AND PERSONS
BY COMMUNITY DISTRICT (CD)
DECEMBER 2002, SEPTEMBER 2004, AND SEPTEMBER 2005

CD	Number of Cases			Number of Persons			Percent Change 12/02 to 9/05		9/04 to 9/05	
	12/02	9/04	9/05	12/04	9/04	9/05	Cases	Persons	Cases	Persons
1	4088	4071	4095	11360	11062	10845	0.2	-4.5	0.6	-2.0
2	1135	1130	1175	2817	2660	2757	3.5	-2.1	4.0	3.6
3	3033	3189	3230	8267	8355	8359	6.5	1.1	1.3	0.0
4	2202	2314	2370	6144	6212	6243	7.6	1.6	2.4	0.5
5	463	403	918	1207	970	2305	98.3	91.0	127.8	137.6
6	416	416	42	879	867	870	1.2	-1.0	1.2	0.3
7	1584	1534	1472	3977	3697	3427	-7.1	-13.8	-4.0	-7.3
8	1056	1055	107	2726	2586	2511	2.1	-7.9	2.2	-2.9
9	1820	1888	1968	5017	5025	5040	8.1	0.5	4.2	0.3
10	2007	1914	1996	5746	5234	5247	-0.5	-8.7	4.3	0.2
11	484	414	408	1267	1018	1000	-15.7	-21.1	-1.4	-1.8
12	9357	8819	9001	25608	22937	22857	-3.8	-10.7	2.1	-0.3
13	2420	2237	2237	6465	5577	5495	-7.6	-15.0	0.0	-1.5
14	3780	3880	4007	11408	11350	11670	6.0	2.3	3.3	2.8
Total	35807	35031	36167	98251	92329	93267	1.0	-5.1	3.2	1.0

15. The community district that had the LARGEST decrease in the number of cases from 12/02 to 9/05 is

A. CD7   B. CD11   C. CD12   D. CD13

16. Which one of the following statements is MOST supported by the chart?

A. CD5 had the largest increase in the number of cases from 12/02 to 9/04.
B. CD5 had the largest decrease in the number of persons on public assistance from 9/04 to 9/05.
C. CD7 had the largest decrease in the number of persons on public assistance from 12/02 to 9/05.
D. CD12 had more than five times the number of cases as CD9 in 9/05.

17. Borough-wide, the total number of persons on public assistance decreased from 12/02 to 9/04 and increased from 9/04 to 9/05.
Which one of the following includes all the community districts which followed this same pattern of change?

A. CD2, CD5, CD6, CD10, CD14
B. CD2, CD5, CD6, CD7, CD14
C. CD2, CD5, CD6, CD12, CD14
D. GD1, CD5, CD5, CD11, CD12

18. During the periods 12/02 to 9/04 and 9/04 to 9/05, how many community districts showed continual increases in both the number of cases and the number of persons receiving public assistance?

    A. 2   B. 3   C. 4   D. 5

Questions 19-22.

DIRECTIONS: Questions 19 through 22 are to be answered SOLELY on the basis of the information contained in the following passage.

The Commissioner and, with the approval of the Commissioner, the Inspectors General and any person under the supervision of the Commissioner or Inspectors General may require any officer or employee of the city to answer questions concerning any matter related to the performance of his or her official duties or any person dealing with the city concerning such dealings with the city, after first being advised that neither their statements nor any information or evidence derived therefrom will be used against them in a subsequent criminal prosecution other than for perjury or contempt arising from such testimony. The refusal of an officer or employee to answer questions on the condition described in this paragraph shall constitute cause for removal from office or employment or other appropriate penalty.

Every officer or employee of the city shall cooperate fully with the Commissioner and the Inspectors General. Interference with or obstruction of an investigation conducted by the Commissioner or an Inspector General shall constitute cause for removal from office or employment or other appropriate penalty.

Every officer and employee of the city shall have the affirmative obligation to report, directly and without undue delay, to the Commissioner or an Inspector General any and all information concerning conduct which they know or should reasonably know to involve corrupt or other criminal activity or conflict of interest, (1) by another city officer or employee, which concerns his or her office or employment, or (2) by persons dealing with the city, which concerns their dealings with the city. The knowing failure of any officer or employee to report as required above shall constitute cause for removal from office or employment or other appropriate penalty.

19. According to the above passage, if a city employee has information concerning criminal wrongdoing by her supervisor in his work with a private agency, she should FIRST

    A. speak with her supervisor about the matter
    B. inform the Inspector General of the information she has
    C. explore the matter further to try to uncover more evidence
    D. speak to her co-workers to determine whether her suspicions are valid

20. Of the following, the passage is MOST concerned with
    A. preventing corrupt or other criminal activity or conflicts of interest in city dealings
    B. establishing what constitutes corrupt or criminal activities by city employees
    C. establishing guidelines for removing city employees from office who do not assist the Inspector General
    D. city employees' responsibilities regarding investigations conducted by the Office of the Inspector General

21. Based on the above passage, it is NOT always necessary to report which one of the following to the Inspector General?
    A. A city employee who accepts a gift from a private business
    B. A private agency whose work for the city presents a conflict of interest
    C. A private vendor who offers a city employee special favors if awarded a city contract
    D. A city employee who conducts private business during his city working hours

22. Of the following, the above passage does NOT discuss the type of penalty a city employee might receive for
    A. intentionally giving misleading answers to questions asked by the Inspector General
    B. criminal actions he committed and which subsequently are uncovered by an investigation of the Inspector General
    C. interfering with an investigation being conducted by the Inspector General
    D. delaying to report corrupt activity to the Inspector General

Questions 23-25.

DIRECTIONS: Questions 23 through 25 are to be answered SOLELY on the basis of the information contained in the following passage.

In 2009, funding for the Older Americans Act programs will be cut by 10% from the 2008 funding levels. There will be 4.6 million dollars less in funds available for congregate and home-delivered meals, employment, and social services for the city's 1.2 million elderly residents. Funding for the Title V Senior Community Services Employment program would be effectively discontinued, resulting in the loss of jobs for 684 elderly persons working in nutrition sites for the elderly, senior centers, day care centers, and hospitals. This job loss would add to the almost 800 jobs in N.Y.C. defunded by the elimination of the Job Opportunity Program. Reductions in the Title IIIC Nutrition and Commodity Foods/cash in lieu programs will jeopardize the delivery of over 500,000 congregate and home-delivered meals annually, and the operation of seven senior citizens centers. Title IIIB services, which include home care, escort, shopping, and transportation services, will be spared in 2009 because of the availability of prior year funds, but will be reduced by nearly one million dollars in 2010, causing the interruption of these supportive services for thousands of elderly persons in the city.

23. According to the information in the above passage, funding cuts for the Title V Senior Community Services Employment program would
    A. not affect the availability of home-delivered meals for the elderly
    B. be greater in 2009 because of an overall decline in the city's population

C. result in the loss of 1,484 jobs for the elderly
D. impact mostly on the staff assigned to senior centers

24. Based on the information in the above passage, which of the following statements is MOST correct? 24._____

    A. Funding cuts will affect only a small portion of the city's elderly population.
    B. The largest funding cuts will take place in Title IIIC programs.
    C. The Job Opportunity Program will not be affected by cuts in Title IIIB programs.
    D. Funding for Older Americans Act programs will be cut by an additional 10% in 2010.

25. Based on the information in the above passage, it can be inferred that escort services for the elderly will 25._____

    A. continue in 2009 but be eliminated in 2010
    B. not be affected in 2010 due to prior year funding
    C. be reduced in 2009 and eliminated in 2010
    D. not be affected in 2009 but reduced in 2010

KEY (CORRECT ANSWERS)

1.	C	11.	B
2.	A	12.	A
3.	B	13.	D
4.	C	14.	C
5.	B	15.	C
6.	D	16.	A
7.	A	17.	A
8.	C	18.	B
9.	D	19.	B
10.	C	20.	D

21.	A
22.	B
23.	A
24.	C
25.	D

EXAMINATION SECTION

TEST 1

DIRECTIONS: Each question or incomplete statement is followed by several suggested answers or completions. Select the one that BEST answers the question or completes the statement. *PRINT THE LETTER OF THE CORRECT ANSWER IN THE SPACE AT THE RIGHT.*

1. The one of the following which would NOT be an appropriate means of ensuring effective community and client participation in program planning and development is
   A. the establishment of citizen advisory committees which include welfare recipients
   B. employment of indigenous community service aides, including recipients
   C. development of appeal and grievance machinery to give client groups access to the administration of the agency
   D. negotiations with staff employee organizations on matters of agency programs

   1.____

2. Representatives of a community organization which has an interest in developing a narcotics service program in a neighborhood with a high rate of narcotics addiction meet with the director of the social services center in order to ask for assistance in developing this program
   The MOST appropriate action for the director to take FIRST would be to
   A. assign a staff member to work with the group
   B. inform the group that development of narcotics service programs is not a responsibility of the Department of Social Services
   C. ask your superior to send a consultant to meet with you in order to develop a plan
   D. inform the group that you cannot refer the matter to the Addiction Services Agency since it is not their responsibility

   2.____

3. Assume that the Department of Social Services has decided to organize local groups to assist in informing the communities of the availability and the nature of services provided under separation of income maintenance from delivery of social services.
   The one of the following which would NOT be an appropriate step to take in order to organize such community groups is to
   A. call a meeting of the representatives of existing community agencies in order to form an advisory committee
   B. ask the neighborhood urban task force to suggest suitable community residents for membership in these groups
   C. make a study in order to obtain relevant facts about the community
   D. identify the informal community power structure

   3.____

4. As a result of a study, private casework Agency X, which has a large center serving your geographical area, has decided to de-emphasize social casework and move into neighborhood organization.
As director of the social services center, the MOST appropriate action for you to take FIRST in order to cooperate with this agency's new program would be
   A. offer to take over the caseload and provide the social services
   B. set up a meeting with the professional leadership of the agency to discuss implications and possible transition of clients into available services
   C. convene the local citizen advisory group and get their reaction to Agency X's decision
   D. purchase casework services for the welfare clients formerly served by Agency X from other voluntary agencies

5. *America's families are in trouble – trouble so deep and pervasive as to threaten the future of our nation*, according to a major report to the White House Conference on Children. Conference participants agreed generally that family life is being weakened by various fundamental changes in American citizens. Many experts believe that the ONLY remaining function that justifies continued support of the family as a social institution is its function as a
   A. medium for the education of children
   B. source of emotional security for family members
   C. means of day-to-day care of children
   D. vehicle for the socialization of its members

6. The administration's proposed Family Assistance Plan was applauded in some quarters because it established the principle of a guaranteed annual income for all Americans. However, many social welfare experts who otherwise favor the guaranteed income principle have voiced criticism of this part of the proposed plan because the
   A. proposed amount of the income guarantee was lower in many states than present welfare benefits
   B. income guarantee was not tied in with a provision that recipients of the guaranteed income are required to work
   C. proposed guaranteed income plan does not consider family composition and family size
   D. lots of welfare recipients in those states which already have comparatively high welfare benefits would have been improved further

7. The Federal Task Force on the Organization of the Social Services has summed up some major principles which should be guidelines in revising the service aspect of the Department of Social Services.
The one of the following which is NOT one of these principles is:
   A. The federal government should assume the entire burden of income maintenance
   B. Consumers should be involved in the planning of services
   C. Services should be directed only to those who are poor or are in danger of becoming poor and eligible for income maintenance
   D. States and local communities should have the option of developing their own style and package of services

8. According to a recent five-year study, the rate of illegitimate births in the United States has nearly doubled during the last decade.
   Of the following, the MOST correct statement about the findings on this problem is that
   A. the basic cause of this increase in the rate of illegitimate births could not be determined
   B. a direct link was found between illegitimacy rates and the number of families receiving welfare benefits
   C. illegitimacy rates were found to be highest in those states with high welfare benefits and lowest in those states with low welfare benefits
   D. there is a significant relationship between inadequate sex education in schools and the rate of illegitimate motherhood among school-age young women

8.____

9. Congressional statutes have extended the Food Stamp program, introducing various changes and policy revisions.
   A SIGNIFICANT change made by Congress is that
   A. college students are ineligible to receive food stamps
   B. recipients of public assistance to not have the option of paying for their food stamps by means of an authorized deduction in their public assistance grant
   C. members of hippie communes are eligible to receive food stamps
   D. employable persons who are not already working are required to register for and accept work in order to be eligible for food stamps

9.____

10. Under a proposed Family Assistance Program, federal grants would be made to the states for individual and family services.
    The one of the following which is a CORRECT statement of the relevant provisions of the proposed program is that the states
    A. would be encouraged to provide individual and family services on the basis of 75% federal reimbursement for specified services, such as child welfare, protective services, family and marriage counseling, and family planning
    B. administering the program must be organizationally connected with the agency administering a cash benefit program on the basis of need
    C. would not be reimbursed by the federal government for foster care for any child for whom a public agency has responsibility
    D. would be discouraged from providing services for low income families above the poverty level in order to forestall dependency

10.____

11. The one of the following statements which MOST accurately characterizes the social services programs developed during the War Against Poverty is:
    A. Priority was given to the opportunity program (e.g., job training education) as contrasted with counseling on personal problems
    B. There was an increasing emphasis on income maintenance programs
    C. There was substantial emphasis on practical or hard social services such as Meals on Wheels and homemaker services
    D. There was a substantial emphasis on soft social services such as family and interpersonal counseling

11.____

12. The State Legislature adopted the so-called flat grant, which provides for a uniform assistance allowance based on family size to meet all needs except for shelter and which eliminated most special allowances.
The one of the following which has NOT occurred as a result of the adoption of the flat grant is:
    A. Improved fiscal control over expenditures made for public assistance because costs can be predicted more accurately
    B. Significant reduction in underpayments and overpayments in computing individual family assistance allowances
    C. Almost no reduction in the number of requests for fair hearings on the grounds of inadequacy of the grant
    D. Facilitation of the individual caseworker's job because of the relative ease in computing the individual family's allowance

13. As a matter of basic state policy, recipients are required to receive their assistance payments in the form of cash. However, it is recognized that under certain specified circumstances, a grant may be restricted in some manner or form because of the circumstances involved.
Restriction of the grant would NOT be appropriate in which one of the following instances?
    A. The cost of care of a recipient's child in a day care center is being met by a payment directly to the center
    B. A landlord decides not to evict a recipient who failed to pay his rent promptly if he receives subsequent rent payment in the form of a vendor payment from the agency
    C. The insurance premiums fall due on a recipient's policy which has been assigned to the agency, and the premium is paid directly to the insurance company
    D. An aged recipient proves incompetent to handle his money, and arrangements are made to have his sister, who lives in the neighborhood, receive his check as a protective payee

14. In order to be eligible for matching federal funds, the state's AABD programs must conform to certain federal requirements which have been laid down by the provisions of the Social Security Act.
The one of the following which is NOT included in the Act is the requirement of
    A. training and effective use of paid sub-professional staff, including recipients and other persons of low income
    B. training and use of unpaid or partially paid volunteers in the provision of services
    C. the use of a simplified statement and method for determining eligibility
    D. separation of income maintenance and service activities into two separate organizational units

15. Of the following, the three groups of welfare recipients which were NOT affected by recent cutbacks are
    A. dependent children, the aged, and those on home relief
    B. The disabled, dependent children, and the blind
    C. The aged, the blind, and those on home relief
    D. The disabled, the aged, and the blind

16. The adoption of the flat grant system by the State Legislature resulted, in part,
    A. as a fulfillment of a federal requirement
    B. as a reaction to overutilization by recipients of their entitlement to special need items
    C. from a recommendation by the Mayor of the City
    D. from negotiations of the union with the Department of Social Services

17. The problem of developing social planning data has been complicated in the city because public agencies have delineated geographic planning or government areas with different boundaries from those used by voluntary or quasi-public organizations.
    To overcome this problem, the city has proposed planning bases which utilize geographic areas comprising the _____ districts.
    A. community planning
    B. elementary school
    C. health
    D. new election

18. The declaration technique as a simplified method of determining eligibility for public assistance has resulted in all of the following EXCEPT
    A. a saving of time and manpower previously spent in verifying information
    B. substantial overall personnel budget savings
    C. speedier delivery of financial assistance to the client
    D. enhancement of the dignity of the client

19. Of the following statements, the one which is MOST representative of the DAB system now operating in the Department of Social Services under separation of income maintenance and delivery services is as follows:
    A. It is organized in such a manner as to provide for the same treatment of short-term and long-term services needs
    B. It is caseload organized for meeting client service needs
    C. The service needs of recipients are met only on request, except when protective services are required
    D. A social study is prepared initially and periodically in order to assess a recipient's need for services

KEY (CORRECT ANSWERS)

1.	D	11.	A
2.	A	12.	A
3.	B	13.	A
4.	B	14.	D
5.	B	15.	D
6.	A	16.	B
7.	C	17.	A
8.	A	18.	B
9.	D	19.	C
10.	A		

TEST 2

DIRECTIONS: Each question or incomplete statement is followed by several suggested answers or completions. Select the one that BEST answers the question or completes the statement. *PRINT THE LETTER OF THE CORRECT ANSWER IN THE SPACE AT THE RIGHT.*

1. With regard to the substantial overall rise in the public assistance caseload in the city in recent years, it would be CORRECT to state that the
    A. rise in the caseload was approximately the same for all categories of assistance
    B. AFDC caseload showed the greatest percentage increase
    C. AABD caseload remained at the same level, despite the overall increase
    D. AD caseload showed the greatest percentage of increase

    1.____

2. During the last few years, the public assistance caseload in the city has substantially increased.
    According to a study of welfare income and employment in the city, the PRINCIPAL reason for this growth is the
    A. break-up of families due to desertion, separation, and other families
    B. higher ate of acceptance of applications
    C. increase in the number of applications for public assistance
    D. migration of families to the city

    2.____

3. There has been considerable debate on alternative methods of giving greater assistance to municipalities because of the rising costs of welfare.
    Many public welfare experts believe that the plan that would be MOST beneficial to the city is
    A. the revenue sharing plan of the administration
    B. the proposal for federalization of DAB and a guaranteed income per family
    C. establishment of a residence requirement to prevent influx of new clients
    D. an increase in the minimum wage

    3.____

4. The concept of advocacy of the client as an important function of the public welfare agency and its staff members can BEST be defined by one of the following? A(n)
    A. contribution of advice and support to the client in his dealings with outside agencies
    B. planned expenditure of effort, professional knowledge and skill in the interests of the client
    C. means of providing legal defense for the client in his dealings with the law and the courts
    D. organized effort to advance a public cause or proposal involving client interests

    4.____

5. Welfare officials have expressed skepticism about the amount of welfare cost that would be saved as a result of a proposal for a one-year residency requirement.
   According to authorities, of the total number of welfare recipients, those with LESS than one-year residency amount to
   A. 1.5%   B. 3%   C. 5%   D. 7.5%

6. Social welfare experts differentiate between the residual and institutional viewpoints as the dominant concepts of social welfare.
   The difference between these concepts can be CORRECTLY described as follows:

	Residual Concept	Institutional Concept
A.	Social welfare is a source of supplementary rehabilitative services to be utilized when regular social processes break down.	Social welfare programs are an integral part and legitimate function of modern society.
B.	The provision of social welfare services is an anomalous function no longer applicable to modern industrial society.	Social welfare programs are land established and a necessary function which is essential to modern life.
C.	The financing of social welfare services is a function which should be the responsibility of federal, state, and the local government.	Social welfare services should be financed by private philanthropic institutions.
D.	The provisions of social welfare services is an essential governmental function and the categorical entitlement of citizens.	Social welfare services are a resource to be utilized only when other institutions are unable to provide these services.

7. Lowering income eligibility for Medicaid would PROBABLY result in a(n)
   A. decrease in welfare costs
   B. increase in the number of welfare recipients
   C. loss of matching federal funds
   D. increase in federal funding

8. AFDC clients generally had a variety of individual and family problems in addition to financial need which require appropriate services.
   A study of the characteristics of AFDC cases in the state revealed that services other than financial assistance received by the LARGEST number of AFDC clients related to
   A. improvement of home and financial management
   B. establishment of paternity
   C. family planning
   D. referral for work or job training

9. The agencies which provide manpower, training, and placement services for public assistance recipients have been severely criticized because of overlapping, poor coordination, and lack of priorities. Suggestions have been made which would eliminate some of these deficiencies.
Of the following, the MOST widely advocated suggestion is:
   A. All vocational training programs presently the responsibility of DHEW should be transferred to the U.S. Department of Labor
   B. Federal funds should be channeled directly to the larger cities in order to minimize the role of state governments in the allocation of funds
   C. A vast system of public employment should be established in order to make the government the employer of last resort
   D. Welfare recipients should be entitled to a top priority in having job training needs met

10. In recent years, while labor unions negotiated substantial contract settlements in most sectors of the economy, the occupations which received the LARGEST percentage of gains were in the
    A. clerical and sales categories
    B. construction industry
    C. professional categories
    D. service industries

11. The requirement of maximum feasible participation of the poor has had a profound influx on anti-poverty programs.
Of the following, the MOST serious problem in fulfilling this requirement has been the
    A. inability to recruit a sufficient number of welfare recipients and indigenous poor who are interested in and capable of involvement in program planning
    B. difficult task of transforming administration in the delivery of social services to achieve client involvement while losing administrative skill and decisiveness
    C. fact that inexperienced poor participants have had a tendency to take control of the programs out of the hands of interested and skillful professionals
    D. creation of antagonism in the middle class communities by aggressive and militant actions organized by welfare recipients and other poor participants

12. Job enlargement, a new approach to raising employee interest and increasing efficiency, is characterized by an increase in the variety of tasks performed by an employee.
The job enlargement approach is designed to
    A. more fully utilize the employee's capabilities, while increasing his responsibilities and according him more freedom of decision
    B. decrease the need for training and for the employee to consult with his peers and superiors
    C. lower the cost of labor and reduce the number of more highly-skilled employees
    D. provide increased employment opportunities for the mentally handicapped and emotionally disturbed

13. As public social service agencies shift their major focus away from eligibility determination, there is the need to develop new priorities, concepts, and techniques in the delivery of social services.
    The one of the following which would NOT be an appropriate aspect of such a program is
    A. decentralization of services
    B. elimination of client information and referral services
    C. client participation in the delivery of services
    D. an interdisciplinary approach in the delivery of services

14. Although large organizations tend to resist change, an organization is MOST likely to change, according to historical evidence, when
    A. it becomes necessary for survival of the organization
    B. the interests of the community at large are at stake
    C. innovations are recommended and approved by administrators and planners
    D. community groups take part in the planning of services

15. Studies have shown that most mentally handicapped can be trained for gainful employment.
    Generally, MOST of the occupations for which they can be trained are classified as
    A. governmental
    B. para-professional
    C. sales and clerical
    D. service

Questions 16-20.

DIRECTIONS: Questions 16 through 20 are to be answered on the basis of the following paragraphs. Based on the information in the paragraphs, mark your answer as follows:
　　A. if only statement I is correct
　　B. if only statement II is correct
　　C. if both statements are correct
　　D. if the excerpts do not contain sufficient evidence for concluding whether either or both statements are correct

　　Almost 49,000 children were living in foster family homes or voluntary institutions in New York State at the end of 2023. These were children whose parents or relatives were unable or unwilling to care for them in their own homes. The New York State Department of Social Services supervised the care of these children served under the auspices of 64 social services districts and more than 150 private agencies and institutions. Almost 8 out of every 1,000 children 18 years of age or younger were in care away from their homes at the end of 2023. This estimate does not include a substantial, but unknown, number of children living outside their own homes who were placed there by their parents, relatives, or others without the assistance of a social agency.

5 (#2)

The number of children in care (dependent, neglected, and delinquent combined) was up by 4,500 or 10 percent over the 2020-2023 period. Both New York City and upstate New York reported similar increases. In the comparable period, New York State's child population (18 years or less) rose only three percent. Thus, the foster care rate showed a moderate increase to 7.7 per thousand in 2023 from 7.2 per thousand in 2020. New York City's foster care rate in 2023, at 10.5 per thousand, was almost twice that for upstate New York, 5.7 per thousand. (Excluding delinquent children from the total in care in the state reduces the foster care rate per thousand to 7.2 in 2023 and the comparable 2020 figure to 6.7.)

Dependent and neglected children made up about 95 percent of the total number in foster family homes and voluntary institutions in New York State at the end of 2023, as they did in 2020. Delinquent children sent into care (outside the state training school system) by the Family Court accounted for only 5 percent of the total. The number of delinquent children in care rose 5 percent, as an increase in upstate New York. 28 percent more than offset a 13 percent decline in New York City. Delinquents comprised 4.9 percent of the total number of children in care upstate at the end of 2023 and 3.9 percent in New York City.

16. I. There were 45,000 children in care away from their own homes over the 2020-2023 period.
    II. The percentage decline of delinquent children in care in New York City in 2023 was offset by a greater increase in the rest of the state.
    The CORRECT answer is:
    A. A   B. B   C. C   D. D

17. I. The increase in delinquent care rate in New York State from 2020 to 2023 cannot be determined from the data given.
    II. New York State's foster care rate in 2023, exclusive of New York City, was about one-half the rate for New York City.
    The CORRECT answer is:
    A. A   B. B   C. C   D. D

18. I. In 2020 and 2023, the percentage of dependent and neglected children in foster family homes and voluntary institutions in New York State was about the same.
    II. In 2020, the number of dependent and neglected children in foster family homes and voluntary institutions in New York State was 43,250.
    The CORRECT answer is:
    A. A   B. B   C. C   D. D

19. I. New York City's child population rose approximately three percent from 2020 to 2023.
    II. At the end of 2023, less than 1% of the children 18 years of age or younger were in care.
    The CORRECT answer is:
    A. A   B. B   C. C   D. D

20. I. Delinquents in New York City comprised 4.4 percent of the total number of children in care in New York City at the end of 2020.
    II. An unsubstantial number of children living outside their own homes were placed by their parents or relatives without the assistance of a social agency.
    The CORRECT answer is:
    A. A   B. B   C. C   D. D

    20.____

KEY (CORRECT ANSWERS)

1.	D	11.	A
2.	C	12.	A
3.	B	13.	B
4.	B	14.	A
5.	A	15.	D
6.	A	16.	B
7.	B	17.	B
8.	A	18.	A
9.	B	19.	D
10.	B	20.	D

EXAMINATION SECTION
TEST 1

DIRECTIONS: Each question or incomplete statement is followed by several suggested answers or completions. Select the one that BEST answers the question or completes the statement. *PRINT THE LETTER OF THE CORRECT ANSWER IN THE SPACE AT THE RIGHT.*

1. In recent years, the social work profession has shifted in emphasis from concern with individual adjustment to concentration on environmental change.
   The one of the following which has NOT generally accompanied this change of emphasis is the

   A. development of new roles for social work professionals
   B. employment of non-professionals in human service organizations
   C. growth of citizen participation in social service programs
   D. determination of the community's appropriate role in relation to the agency's stage of development

2. The reporting system known as the Social Services Information System (SSIS) is BEST described as a method of

   A. determining how direct-service staff allocate their time in relation to defined productivity measures and operating costs
   B. defining the work of a public social service agency in terms of services, elements, activities, and costs
   C. evaluating performance of staff in terms of how they allocate their time in relation to defined productivity measures
   D. determining costs for individual cases in terms of how staff allocate their time to related services, elements, and activities

3. The one of the following which is NOT a major purpose of the Social Services Information System (SSIS) is the provision of information useful in determining

   A. trends in clientele
   B. quality of service
   C. shifts in service demands
   D. service priorities

4. The system of reporting delivery of services under Goal-Oriented Social Services (GOSS) DIFFERS from the reporting requirements introduced by the 1962 Social Security amendments in that the focus of GOSS is in the

   A. objectives of specific areas of services delivery
   B. service plan for the client and the overall, long-term case purpose
   C. allocation of resources
   D. objectives set by the caseworker rather than the client

5. In the language of social service programming, case accountability means MOST NEARLY

   A. departmental responsibility for costs of all services provided for children, adult clients, and families
   B. continuing responsibility for service to a family until the case is closed

C. organizational autonomy for those services the particular organization provides for children, adults, and families
D. departmental responsibility to the consumer and the public for providing needed services

6. After years of controversy, family planning services are now being supported by sound fiscal backing and federal mandate.
According to current requirements, family planning services must be made available to ALL

   A. persons requesting such services
   B. persons 14 years of age and over
   C. female heads of households
   D. women of child-bearing age

7. Research studies indicate that, of the following, the basic strength of a community program sponsored by a public or voluntary agency depends MOST directly on the

   A. enlistment of support from representative minority community leaders
   B. degree of understanding by professional community organization workers of the life-style of community residents
   C. ability of community organization workers to help disadvantaged community members develop their feelings of self-worth
   D. complete control by indigenous people of decision-making and operation of the program

8. Which of the following developments would have the MOST significant impact on the current trend toward decentralization in the delivery of social services?
   A. Action by the U.S. Congress which would reduce the number of federally mandated social services
   B. Takeover by the State Department of Social Services of some aspects of the medical assistance program
   C. Participation by the Community Development Agency with the Department of Social Services in planning for community social services
   D. amendments to the Social Security Act assigning responsibility to the states for definition of services, eligibility standards, and regulations

9. When the AFDC mother's youngest child becomes eighteen, the mother is no longer eligible to receive AFDC benefits. A problem equal in magnitude to the problems of job scarcity and lack of training opportunities is the unreadiness of some of these women to move into the competitive labor market.
The one of the following which would be the MOST appropriate suggestion to help increase the motivation of AFDC mothers to become self-dependent is the establishment of

   A. cash stipends to AFDC mothers who participate in training programs
   B. therapeutic groups to help AFDC mothers develop confidence and self-esteem
   C. a food stamp bonus system for AFDC mothers who accept job offers
   D. special community-based centers for individual job counselling of AFDC mothers

10. The one of the following which is NOT generally considered to be a function of the community social worker is to

   A. act as a catalyst for the organization or community groups
   B. provide leadership in identifying community needs
   C. arrange group programs such as group counselling and consumer education
   D. give *in-depth* casework service to community residents

11. Of the following, the OLDEST original model for social work practice is

   A. group treatment
   B. milieu therapy
   C. task and situational strategy
   D. social diagnosis

12. The term *diagnosis,* as used in social work, USUALLY refers to the worker's
   A. professional assessment as to the nature of the need or the problem which the client presents
   B. identification of mental illness by investigation of its symptoms and its history
   C. recommendation as to the treatment plan for the client on the basis of his problems
   D. categorization of the individual client according to a functional classification of psycho-social problems

13. The aim of crisis intervention and treatment as a model of social work practice is to
   A. give the most help to individuals who view a crisis as a challenge rather than a threat
   B. restore the person to the level of functioning he was able to reach before the crisis occurred, and help him achieve more effective functioning if possible
   C. assess the state of crisis and the person's capacity to cope with the situation
   D. make an objective determination of the reality of the crisis in terms of the person's life situation in order to help him develop new adaptive mechanisms

14. The traditional unit of attention in social casework has been the

   A. client's environment and economic situation
   B. person-in-situation configuration
   C. opportunity systems available to the client
   D. person's ability to overcome his problems

15. The one of the following which is GENERALLY considered to be a basic purpose of the separation of income maintenance and social services is to

   A. maximize the client's choices and control over his own affairs
   B. establish more efficient methods of eligibility determination
   C. encourage community participation in the delivery of social services
   D. reduce the need for workers with college degrees and professional social work training

16. The current Federal effort to retrench on the funding of social services is accompanied by considerable debate over the merits of *hard* vs. *soft* services.
   The one of the following which can be classified as a *soft* service is

   A. child care for working mothers   C. physical therapy
   B. family planning   D. rehabilitation

17. Social work profession has developed in a pattern that is quite different from other professions in that the emphasis in social work practice has changed from _____ to _____.

    A. generalist; specialist
    B. specialist; generalist
    C. activist; reformer
    D. counselor; therapist

18. Senior citizens require a variety of services to enable them to cope effectively with physical and psychological changes and the loss of social contacts.
    Of the following services, senior citizen centers can be MOST useful for providing elderly clients with

    A. protective care
    B. vocational therapy
    C. health services and nutrition education
    D. new identifications, roles, and relationships

19. Services to alcoholics and drug abusers have been expanded to include many different types of treatment modalities. However, experts generally agree that an ESSENTIAL element of any successful treatment plan is

    A. psychoactive medication
    B. deterrent therapy
    C. individual and/or group counselling
    D. family counselling

20. Protective services in child abuse cases are now directed towards improving and strengthening positive functioning in the child's own family in order to avoid the destructive effects of separation of the child from the family. Which of the following treatment modalities would offer the GREATEST potential for success in achieving this objective?

    A. Frequent regular psychotherapy sessions for the abusing parent while the child remains at home
    B. Family counselling of the parents and siblings while the child is temporarily placed in foster care
    C. Daytime child care services for the abused child, combined with therapeutic group services for the parents
    D. Admission of the abused child to a day care center and regular psychiatric treatment of the abusing parent

21. A recent study of multi-problem families on public assistance in the city of Baltimore gives evidence that individuals and families who are most seriously in need of social services are least likely to take the initiative to ask for services.
    Of the following services, this finding has the MOST significant implications for the current public welfare policy and practice of

    A. goal-oriented social services
    B. separation of income maintenance and social services
    C. decentralization of service delivery
    D. work relief employment services

22. The State Task Force on Welfare and Social Services, known as the Scott Commission, focused PRIMARILY on the

    A. administration of financial assistance
    B. delivery of social services
    C. elimination of welfare fraud
    D. State take-over of income support operations

23. Separation of the income maintenance and social services functions originated from action by the

    A. U.S. Congress
    B. State Department of Social Services
    C. U.S. Department of Health, Education and Welfare
    D. Human Resources Administration

24. The supervisor should be familiar with many statutes, rules, and regulations for administration of care of children at public expense.
    Which of the following would be LEAST relevant to his work?

    A. Social Welfare Law
    B. Rules and Regulations of H.E.W.
    C. Rules and Regulations of the State Board and State Department of Social Services
    D. The Family Court Act of NY State

25. Assume that a supervisor is reviewing a sample of case records in order to evaluate the effectiveness of his subordinates' service to clients.
    Of the following, the BEST indication that a worker is making effective referrals of clients to other community agencies would be when the case record shows that the

    A. client has participated in the decision to make the contact with the other agency
    B. caseworker has no further contact with the other agency after the initial referral
    C. client has no further contact with the caseworker after keeping his appointment with the other agency
    D. caseworker visits the other agency before making referrals

KEY (CORRECT ANSWERS)

1. D
2. A
3. B
4. B
5. B

6. B
7. C
8. D
9. B
10. D

11. D
12. A
13. B
14. B
15. A

16. C
17. B
18. D
19. C
20. C

21. B
22. B
23. C
24. B
25. A

TEST 2

DIRECTIONS: Each question or incomplete statement is followed by several suggested answers or completions. Select the one that BEST answers the question or completes the statement. *PRINT THE LETTER OF THE CORRECT ANSWER IN THE SPACE AT THE RIGHT.*

1. Of the following, a SIGNIFICANT criticism recently made of the separation of income maintenance and social services is that services are separated without

    A. requiring periodic diagnosis of clients' problems
    B. directing clients to accept services
    C. offering referrals to private agencies
    D. making clients responsible for recognizing their needs for services

    1._____

2. The MAIN source of the salaries of public assistance clients who are placed in city jobs through the Work Relief Employment Program is

    A. city capital budget funds
    B. federal appropriations
    C. state appropriations
    D. welfare funds

    2._____

3. Photo ID cards, required for public assistance recipients by State regulations, were INITIALLY proposed for the purpose of

    A. locating ineligibles
    B. protecting clients
    C. recertification of clients
    D. reducing case load growth

    3._____

4. A significant aspect of the general revenue sharing bill (P.L. 92-512) which has a direct impact on the expansion of social services programs is the tendency of this legislation to

    A. shift decision-making authority to states and localities and reduce federal responsibility for solutions to economic and social problems
    B. give states and localities unrestricted use of revenue-sharing funds for expenditures without considering specified priority areas
    C. give the federal government tighter control over revenue-sharing funds used to establish and expand social service programs
    D. allocate decision-making authority to states and localities on the basis of population as indicated by census figures

    4._____

5. Which of the following is a present trend in community social services for the disadvantaged concurrent with the separation of income maintenance and social services?

    A. Emphasis on family functioning
    B. Lowered status of the social work professional
    C. Differential use of income maintenance staff
    D. Elimination of eligibility verification

    5._____

6. The Office of the Welfare Inspector-General, which was established in response to criticism of the efficiency of state and local operations in public assistance eligibility determinations, was assigned the function of

    A. quality control of eligibility decisions
    B. registry and location of deserting parents
    C. investigation of fraud in local center operations
    D. welfare check reconciliation

    6._____

7. The food stamp program, which was designed to help increase the purchasing power of low-income persons, has been only minimally used by those whom it is supposed to benefit.
   The one of the following which is NOT a plausible reason for the present underutilization of food stamps is that
   A. low-income people do not understand the program or the benefits of the bonus system
   B. the recipient's neighbors, store clerks, and casual acquaintances have the opportunity to know that they are getting government aid
   C. information about the program is channeled through institutional sources to the largest number of people who use the program
   D. participation is discouraged because of the cumbersome administrative structure of the food stamp distribution system

8. State and city public welfare officials have instituted several new administrative procedures in their efforts to insure the eligibility of the ADC caseload.
   Which of the following is NOT one of these procedures?
   A. Face-to-face recertification
   B. Photo identification cards
   C. Mandatory registration with the state employment service
   D. Mailings to verify current address and eligibility status

9. A major organizational change became effective during the seventies, when responsibility for financial aid to disabled, aged, and blind clients was transferred from the Human Resources Administration to the Social Security Administration.
   Which of the following responsibilities to DAB clients continues to be carried out by the Human Resources Administration?
   A. Eligibility certification
   B. Provision of social services
   C. Medical assistance
   D. Special grants

10. Of the following, the MOST serious problem that has developed as a result of the changeover to the Federal Supplemental Security Income program for the aged and disabled is the
    A. reduction of income for many aged recipients
    B. breakdown between income maintenance and services within the SSI formula
    C. required provision of social services to disabled recipients
    D. disqualification of alcoholics and drug addicts as *disabled* persons eligible for benefits

11. The effect of the recent increase in Social Security benefits on aged recipients of the Supplemental Security Income program has been to
    A. increase their net benefits
    B. leave their net benefits unchanged.
    C. increase benefits for those who are disabled
    D. raise their support levels

12. United States Supreme Court decisions regarding welfare rights, Jefferson vs. Hackney (1972) and Rosado vs. Wyman (1970), were IMPORTANT cases for comparison because both cases deal with the

   A. *substitute father* rule
   B. cost of living provision
   C. residence requirement
   D. mandatory home visits provision

12._____

13. The lawsuit, Wilder vs. Sugarman, alleged that the existing statutory base for the provision of child welfare services in New York City is unconstitutional. The suit sought to obtain a court order forcing the government agencies named in the petition to develop a plan for a new system of publicly supported child-welfare services to meet the present-day needs of children and families. The BASIC issue involved in this case is

   A. direct vs. purchased services for children in need of placement
   B. discrimination against black children by private adoption agencies
   C. the requirement of child placement according to race
   D. discrimination against black children in need of services

13._____

14. A recent article in a professional journal reported that narcotics addicts make up 10 percent of the welfare population, yet account for fully 50 percent of all transactions in the centers. The one of the following which is NOT a plausible reason for this situation is that

   A. services to narcotics addicts are more difficult and time-consuming than services to other clients
   B. narcotics addicts must be served by selecting a group of specially trained workers
   C. workers must devote more time to medical and psychiatric referrals for narcotics addicts
   D. necessary investigation of criminal activity of narcotics addicts is lengthy and difficult

14._____

15. The incremental approach has recently been discussed in the press as a preferable strategy for welfare reform at this period in history.
   The one of the following which is NOT an example of the incremental approach to welfare reform is the

   A. addition of a housing allowance for low-income persons and the use of this new benefit as the key to improvement of other programs
   B. provision of a work bonus to effect program reform and integration
   C. introduction of a negative income tax and a comprehensive new welfare program to replace most existing programs
   D. expansion of food stamp benefits and addition of a cost-of-living escalation provision

15._____

16. Of the following, generally the MOST crucial factor which may limit or prevent community participation in social service programs for the disadvantaged is the

   A. middle-class citizen's fear of reinforcing corrupt lifestyles
   B. taxpayers' demands for greater government economy and efficiency
   C. depersonalization and categorization of public assistance clients
   D. inherent inequality between the social work professional and the client

16._____

17. Administrators of social programs are in general agreement that public participation is a practical and necessary part of the effective implementation of social policy.
In order to ensure optimum public participation in making decisions on the size of public assistance allotments, it would be PARTICULARLY important to

   A. allow a majority of the organized welfare recipients to determine the size of the allotments
   B. achieve the proper combination of checks and balances among the various segments of the population relevant to the decision on the size of the allotments
   C. provide for ongoing, continuous decision-making on public assistance allotments by the taxpaying public who finance these payments
   D. make official liaison, concurrence, consultation, and policy-making the responsibilities of the client population

18. Effective community participation to ensure social justice for minorities does not flow automatically from more or maximum participation of individuals.
Of the following, this statement implies MOST NEARLY that

   A. effective participation requires both professional leadership and numerical strength
   B. democratic participation is not synonymous with majority rule
   C. effective participation is determined by the number of decisions made
   D. majority rule is the best means of obtaining social justice for minority groups

19. Experts generally agree that decisions on the social services to be minimally provided must be the result of city-wide centralized coordinated planning by a joint council with public, voluntary agency and community representation.
The one of the following which would NOT be a desirable result of such coordinated effort is

   A. avoidance of gaps and duplication of services
   B. universality of essential and mandated services
   C. uniformity of services at the community level
   D. minimal waste of resources

20. The one of the following elements which is MOST crucial to the success of a community social services operation is

   A. the employment of indigenous paraprofessionals
   B. operation of a day care service on the premises
   C. a carefully developed intake process
   D. centralized preliminary screening unit

21. Questions have been raised about the popular assumption that the special advantage of employing indigenous paraprofessionals in social work and mental health agencies is their similarity in background and abilities to the clients of the agency.
The BASIS for questioning this assumption is the finding that community people who serve as paraprofessionals

   A. tend to be better educated, more successful, and more upwardly mobile than their neighbors
   B. are unable to be objective about their neighbors' situation and needs because of the similarity to their own problems
   C. are more likely to be naive and to allow themselves to be manipulated by the clients
   D. tend to have inadequate education and lack of ambition and aspiration

22. The Human Resources Administration has a commitment to make extensive use of voluntary and community-based organizations as contractors to provide services to clients. One of the characteristics of a *voluntary,* in contrast to a *community-based* organization, is that a *voluntary* organization is

22._____

A. administered mainly by professionally-trained staff
B. sponsored and staffed mainly by volunteers
C. sponsored by community residents and staffed mainly by non-professionals
D. established mainly by means of public funding

23. Decentralization of services into the neighborhoods has been a key feature of the organization of the Human Resources Administration during the past few years. However, the need has recently emerged for a kind of agency which can provide services most effectively on a city-wide, rather than a neighborhood, basis for

23._____

A. persons recently discharged from state institutions
B. members of other ethnic groups residing in areas largely populated by blacks
C. middle-class residents of Human Resources Districts eligible for child welfare services
D. narcotics addicts

24. A basic problem in the reorganization of the Department of Social Services for separation of income maintenance and service functions has been providing access to the service system.
Which of the following would probably be the MOST productive means of encouraging clients to use available social services?

24._____

A. Outreach activities by the Community Development Agency
B. Referrals from income maintenance workers
C. Referrals from other public and private agencies
D. Neighborhood-based information and referral centers

25. Of the following, the MOST crucial step in clarifying long-range community strategy to develop coordinated public and privately sponsored social services should be

25._____

A. emphasis on functions rather than agencies
B. definition of the functions of individual agencies
C. limitation of the functions of a given agency
D. community assignment of functions to each agency

KEY (CORRECT ANSWERS)

1.	A	11.	B
2.	D	12.	B
3.	B	13.	D
4.	A	14.	B
5.	A	15.	C
6.	C	16.	B
7.	C	17.	B
8.	C	18.	B
9.	B	19.	C
10.	B	20.	C

21. A
22. A
23. B
24. D
25. A

EXAMINATION SECTION
TEST 1

DIRECTIONS: Each question or incomplete statement is followed by several suggested answers or completions. Select the one that BEST answers the question or completes the statement. *PRINT THE LETTER OF THE CORRECT ANSWER IN THE SPACE AT THE RIGHT.*

1. One of the responsibilities of the supervisor is to provide top administration with information about clients and their problems that will help in the evaluation of existing policies and indicate the need for modifications. In order to fulfill this responsibility, it would be MOST essential for the supervisor to

    A. routinely forward all regularly prepared and recurrent reports from his subordinates to his immediate superior
    B. regularly review agency rules, regulations, and policies to make sure that he has sufficient knowledge to make appropriate analyses
    C. note repeated instances of failure of staff to correctly administer a policy and schedule staff conferences for corrective training
    D. analyze reports on cases submitted by subordinates in order to select relevant trend material to be forwarded to his superiors

1.____

2. You find that your division has a serious problem because of unusually long delays in filing reports and overdue approvals to private agencies under contract for services. The MOST appropriate step to take FIRST in this situation would be to

    A. request additional staff to work on reports and approvals
    B. order staff to work overtime until the backlog is eliminated
    C. impress staff with the importance of expeditious handling of reports and approvals
    D. analyze present procedures for handling reports and approvals

2.____

3. When a supervisor finds that he must communicate orally information that is significant enough to affect the entire staff, it would be MOST important to

    A. distribute a written summary of the information to his staff before discussing it orally
    B. tell his subordinate supervisors to discuss this information at individual conferences with their subordinates
    C. call a follow-up meeting of absentees as soon as they return
    D. restate and summarize the information in order to make sure that everyone understands its meaning and implications

3.____

4. Of the following, the BEST way for a supervisor to assist a subordinate who has unusually heavy work pressures is to

    A. point out that such pressures go with the job and must be tolerated
    B. suggest to him that the pressures probably result from poor handling of his workload
    C. help him to be selective in deciding on priorities during the period of pressure
    D. ask him to work overtime until the period of pressure is over

4.____

5. Leadership is a basic responsibility of the supervisor. The one of the following which would be the LEAST appropriate way to fulfill this role is for the supervisor to

    A. help staff to work up to their capacities in every possible way
    B. encourage independent judgment and actions by staff members
    C. allow staff to participate in decisions within policy limits
    D. take over certain tasks in which he is more competent than his subordinates

6. Assume that you have assigned a very difficult administrative task to one of your best subordinate supervisors, but he is reluctant to take it on because he fears that he will fail in it. It is your judgment, however, that he is quite capable of performing this task.
The one of the following which is the MOST desirous way for you to handle this situation is to

    A. reassure him that he has enough skill to perform the task and that he will not be penalized if he fails
    B. reassign the task to another supervisor who is more achievement-oriented and more confident of his skills
    C. minimize the importance of the task so that he will feel it is safe for him to attempt it
    D. stress the importance of the task and the dependence of the other staff members on his succeeding in it

7. Assume that a member of your professional staff deliberately misinterprets a new state directive because he fears that its enforcement will have an adverse effect on clients. Although you consider him to be a good supervisor and basically agree with him, you should direct him to comply. Of the following, the MOST desirable way for you to handle this situation would be to

    A. avoid a confrontation with him by transferring responsibility for carrying out the directive to another member of your staff
    B. explain to him that you are in a better position than he to assess the implications of the new directive
    C. discuss with him the basic reasons for his misinterpretation and explain why he must comply with the directive
    D. allow him to interpret the directive in his own way as long as he assumes full responsibility for his actions

8. Of the following, the MAIN reason it is important for an administrator in a large organization to properly coordinate the work delegated to subordinates is that such coordination

    A. makes it unnecessary to hold frequent staff meetings and conferences with key staff members
    B. reduces the necessity for regular evaluation of procedures and programs, production, and performance of personnel
    C. results in greater economy and stricter accountability for the organization's resources
    D. facilitates integration of the contributions of the numerous staff members who are responsible for specific parts of the total workload

9. The one of the following which would NOT be an appropriate reason for the formulation of an entirely new policy is that it would

A. serve as a positive affirmation of the agency's function and how it is to be carried out
B. give focus and direction to the work of the staff, particularly in decision-making
C. inform the public of the precise conditions under which services will be rendered
D. provide procedures which constitute uniform methods of carrying out operations

10. Of the following, it is MOST difficult to formulate policy in an organization where

    A. work assignments are narrowly specialized by units
    B. staff members have varied backgrounds and a wide range of competency
    C. units implementing the same policy are in the same geographic location
    D. staff is experienced and fully trained

11. For a supervisor to feel that he is responsible for influencing the attitudes of his staff members is GENERALLY considered

    A. *undesirable;* attitudes of adults are emotional factors which usually cannot be changed
    B. *desirable;* certain attitudes can be obstructive and should be modified in order to provide effective service to clients
    C. *undesirable;* the supervisor should be nonjudgmental and accepting of widely different attitudes and social patterns of staff members
    D. *desirable;* influencing attitudes is a teaching responsibility which the supervisor shares with the training specialist

12. The one of the following which is NOT generally a function of the higher-level supervisor is

    A. projecting the budget and obtaining financial resources
    B. providing conditions conducive to optimum employee production
    C. maintaining records and reports as a basis for accountability and evaluation
    D. evaluating program achievements and personnel effectiveness in accordance with goals and standards

13. As a supervisor in a recently decentralized services center offering multiple services, you are given responsibility for an orientation program for professional staff on the recent reorganization of the department.
    Of the following, the MOST appropriate step to take FIRST would be to

    A. organize a series of workshops for subordinate supervisors
    B. arrange a tour of the new geographic area of service
    C. review supervisors' reports, statistical data, and other relevant material
    D. develop a resource manual for staff on the reorganized center

14. Experts generally agree that the content of training sessions should be closely related to workers' practice. Of the following, the BEST method of achieving this aim is for the training conference leader to

    A. encourage group discussion of problems that concern staff in their practice
    B. develop closer working relationships with top administration
    C. coordinate with central office to obtain feedback on problems that concern staff
    D. observe workers in order to develop a pattern of problems for class discussion

15. The one of the following which is generally the MOST useful teaching tool for professional staff development is

    A. visual aids and tape recordings
    B. professional literature
    C. agency case material
    D. lectures by experts

16. The one of the following which is NOT a good reason for using group conferences as a method of supervision is to

    A. give workers a feeling of mutual support through sharing common problems
    B. save time by eliminating the need for individual conferences
    C. encourage discussion of certain problems that are not as likely to come up in individual conferences
    D. provide an opportunity for developing positive identification with the department and its programs

17. The supervisor, in his role as teacher, applies his teaching in line with his understanding of people and realizes that teaching is a highly individualized process, based on understanding of the worker as a person and as a learner.
    This statement implies MOST NEARLY that the supervisor must help the worker to

    A. overcome his biases
    B. develop his own ways of working
    C. gain confidence in his ability
    D. develop the will to work

18. Of the following, the circumstances under which it would be MOST appropriate to divide a training conference for professional staff into small workshops is when

    A. some of the trainees are not aware of the effect of their attitudes and behavior on others
    B. the trainees need to look at human relations problems from different perspectives
    C. the trainees are faced with several substantially different types of problems in their job assignments
    D. the trainees need to know how to function in many different capacities

19. Of the following, the MAIN reason why it is important to systematically evaluate a specific training program while it is in progress is to

    A. collect data that will serve as a valid basis for improving the agency's overall training program and maintaining control over its components
    B. insure that instruction by training specialists is conducted in a manner consistent with the planned design of the training program
    C. identify areas in which additional or remedial training for the training specialists can be planned and implemented
    D. provide data which are usable in effecting revisions of specific components of the training program

20. Staff development has been defined as an educational process which seeks to provide agency staff with knowledge about specific job responsibilities and to effect changes in staff attitudes and behavior patterns. Assume that you are assigned to define the educational objectives of a specific training program.
In accordance with the above concept, the MOST helpful formulation would be a statement of the

   A. purpose and goals of each training session
   B. generalized patterns of behavior to be developed in the trainees
   C. content material to be presented in the training sessions
   D. kind of behavior to be developed in the trainees and the situations in which this behavior will be applied

20.____

21. In teaching personnel under your supervision how to gather and analyze facts before attempting to solve a problem, the one of the following training methods which would be MOST effective is

   A. case study
   B. role playing
   C. programmed learning
   D. planned experience

21.____

22. Federal and state welfare agencies have been discussing the importance of analyzing functions traditionally included in the position of caseworker, with a view toward identifying and separating those activities to be performed by the most highly skilled personnel.
Of the following, an IMPORTANT secondary gain which can result from such differential use of staff is that

   A. supporting job assignments can be given to persons unable to meet the demands of casework, to the satisfaction of all concerned
   B. documentation will be provided on workers who are not suited for all the duties now part of the caseworker's job
   C. caseworkers with a high level of competence in working with people can be rewarded through promotion or merit increases
   D. incompetent workers can be identified and categorized as a basis for transfer or separation from the service

22.____

23. Of the following, a serious DISADVANTAGE of a performance evaluation system based on standardized evaluation factors is that such a system tends to

   A. exacerbate the anxieties of those supervisors who are apprehensive about determining what happens to another person
   B. subject the supervisor to psychological stress by emphasizing the incompatibility of his dual role as both judge and counselor
   C. create organizational conflict by encouraging personnel who wish to enhance their standing to become too aggressive in the performance of their duties
   D. lead many staff members to concentrate on measuring up in terms of the evaluation factors and to disregard other aspects of their work

23.____

24. Which of the following would contribute MOST to the achievement of conformity of staff activities and goals to the intent of agency policies and procedures?

   A. Effective communications and organizational discipline
   B. Changing nature of the underlying principles and desired purpose of the policies and procedures

24.____

C. Formulation of specific criteria for implementing the policies and procedures
D. Continuous monitoring of the essential effectiveness of agency operations

25. Job enlargement, a management device used by large organizations to counteract the adverse effects of specialization on employee performance, is LEAST likely to improve employee motivation if it is accomplished by

   A. lengthening the job cycle and adding a large number of similar tasks
   B. allowing the employee to use a greater variety of skills
   C. increasing the scope and complexity of the employee's job
   D. giving the employee more opportunities to make decisions

KEY (CORRECT ANSWERS)

1.	D	11.	B
2.	D	12.	A
3.	D	13.	A
4.	C	14.	A
5.	D	15.	C
6.	A	16.	B
7.	C	17.	B
8.	D	18.	C
9.	D	19.	A
10.	B	20.	D

21. A
22. A
23. D
24. A
25. A

TEST 2

DIRECTIONS: Each question or incomplete statement is followed by several suggested answers or completions. Select the one that BEST answers the question or completes the statement. *PRINT THE LETTER OF THE CORRECT ANSWER IN THE SPACE AT THE RIGHT.*

1. When a supervisor requires approval for case action on a higher level, the process used is known as

   A. administrative clearance
   B. going outside channels
   C. administrative consultation
   D. delegation of authority

   1.____

2. In delegating authority to his subordinates, the one of the following to which a good supervisor should give PRIMARY consideration is the

   A. results expected of them
   B. amount of power to be delegated
   C. amount of responsibility to be delegated
   D. their skill in the performance of present tasks

   2.____

3. Of the following, the type of decision which could be SAFELY delegated to lower-level staff without undermining basic supervisory responsibility is one which

   A. involves a commitment that can be fulfilled only over a long period of time
   B. has fairly uncertain goals and promises
   C. has the possibility of modification built into it
   D. may generate considerable resistance from those affected by it

   3.____

4. Of the following, the MOST valuable contribution made by the informal organization in a large public service agency is that such an organization

   A. has goals and values which are usually consistent with and reinforce those of the formal organization
   B. is more flexible than the formal organization and more adaptable to changing conditions
   C. has a communications system which often contributes to the efficiency of the formal organization
   D. represents a sound basis on which to build the formal organizational structure

   4.____

5. Of the following, the condition under which it would be MOST useful for a social services agency to develop detailed procedures is when

   A. subordinate supervisory personnel need a structure to help them develop greater independence
   B. employees have little experience or knowledge of how to perform certain assigned tasks
   C. coordination of agency activities is largely dependent upon personal contact
   D. agency activities must continually adjust to changes in local circumstances

   5.____

6. Assume that a certain public agency administrator has the management philosophy that his agency's responsibility is to routinize existing operations, meet each day's problems as they arise, and resolve problems with a minimun of residual effect upon himself or his agency.
The possibility that this official would be able to administer his agency without running into serious difficulties would be MORE likely during a period of

   A. economic change
   B. social change
   C. economic crisis
   D. social and economic stability

7. Some large organizations have adopted the practice of allowing each employee to establish his own performance goals, and then later evaluate himself in an individual conference with his immediate supervisor.
Of the following, a DRAWBACK of this approach is that the employee

   A. may set his goals too low and rate himself too highly
   B. cannot control those variables which may improve his performance
   C. has no guidelines for improving his performance
   D. usually finds it more difficult to criticize himself than to accept criticism from others

8. Decentralization of services cannot completely eliminate the requirement of central office approval for certain case actions.
The MOST valid reason for complaint about this requirement is that

   A. unavoidable delay created by referral to central office may cause serious problems for the client
   B. it may lower morals of supervisors who are not given the authority to take final action on urgent cases
   C. the concept of role responsibility is minimized
   D. the objective of delegated responsibility tends to be negated

9. Which of the following would be the MOST useful administrative tool for the purpose of showing the sequence of operations and staff involved?
A(n)

   A. organization chart
   B. flow chart
   C. manual of operating procedures
   D. statistical review

10. The prevailing pattern of organization in large public agencies consists of a limited span of control and organization by function or, at lower levels, process.
Of the following, the PRINCIPAL effect which this pattern or organization has on the management of work is that it

    A. reduces the management burden in significant ways
    B. creates a time lag between the perception of a problem and action on it
    C. makes it difficult to direct and observe employee performance
    D. facilitates the development of employees with managerial ability

11. The one of the following which would be the MOST appropriate way to reduce tensions between line and staff personnel in public service agencies is to

    A. provide in-service training that will increase the sensitivity of line and staff personnel to their respective roles
    B. assign to staff personnel the role of providing assistance only when requested by line personnel
    C. separate staff from line personnel and provide staff with its own independent reward structure
    D. give line and staff personnel equal status in making decisions

12. In determining the appropriate span of control for subordinate supervisors, which of the following principles should be followed?
    The more

    A. complex the work, the broader the effective span of control
    B. similar the jobs being supervised, the more narrow the effective span of control
    C. interdependent the jobs being supervised, the more narrow the effective span of control
    D. unpredictable the work, the broader the effective span of control

13. A method sometimes used in public service agencies to improve upward communication is to require subordinate supervisory staff to submit to top management monthly narrative reports of any problems which they deem important for consideration.
    Of the following, a MAJOR disadvantage of this method is that it may

    A. enable subordinate supervisors to avoid thinking about their problems by simply referring such matters to their superiors
    B. obscure important issues so that they are not given appropriate attention
    C. create a need for numerous staff conferences in order to handle all of the reported problems
    D. encourage some subordinate supervisors to focus on irrelevant matters and compete with each other in the length and content of their reports

14. The use of a committee as an approach to the problem of coordinating interdepartmental activities can present difficulties if the committee functions PRIMARILY as a(n)

    A. means of achieving personal objectives and goals
    B. instrument for coordinating activities that flow across departmental lines
    C. device for involving subordinate personnel in the decision-making process
    D. means of giving representation to competing interest groups

15. A study was recently made of the attitudes and perceptions of a sample of public assistance workers in nine New Jersey county welfare boards who had experienced a major organizational change and redefinition of their jobs as a result of separation of the income maintenance and social services functions. Questionnaires administered to these workers indicated that a disproportionate number of workers in the larger agencies were dissatisfied with the reorganization and their new assignments. Of the following, the MOST plausible reason for this dissatisfaction is that workers in larger agencies are

A. less likely to be known to management and to be personally disciplined if they expressed dissatisfaction with their new roles
B. less likely to have the opportunity to participate in planning a reorganization and to be given consideration for the assignments they preferred
C. given a shorter lead period to implement the change and, therefore, had insufficient time to plan the reorganization and carry it out efficiently
D. usually made up of more older members who have had routinized their work according to habit and find it more difficult to adjust to change

16. An article which recently appeared in a professional journal presents a proposal for participatory leadership in which the goal of supervision would be development of subordinates' self-reliance, with the premise that each staff member is held accountable for his own performance. The one of the following which would NOT be a desirable outcome of this type of supervision is the

    A. necessity for subordinates to critically examine their performance
    B. development by some subordinates of skills not possessed by the supervisor
    C. establishment of a quality control unit for sample checking and identification of errors
    D. relaxation of demands made on the supervisor

17. The *management by objectives* concept is a major development in the administration of human services organizations. The purpose of this approach is to establish a system for

    A. reduction of waiting time
    B. planning and controlling work output
    C. consolidation of organizational units
    D. work measurement

18. Assume that you encounter a serious administrative problem in implementing a new program. After consulting with members of your staff individually, you come up with several alternate solutions.
    Of the following, the procedure which would be MOST appropriate for evaluating the relative merits of each solution would be to

    A. try all of them on a limited experimental basis
    B. break the problem down into its component parts and analyze the effect of each solution on each component in terms of costs and benefits
    C. break the problem down into its component parts, eliminate all intangibles, and measure the effect of the tangible aspects of each solution on each component in terms of costs and benefits
    D. bring the matter before your weekly staff conference, discuss the relative merits of each alternate solution, and then choose the one favored by the majority of the conference

19. When establishing planning objectives for a service program under your supervision, the one of the following principles which should be followed is that objectives

    A. are rarely verifiable if they are qualitative
    B. should be few in number and of equal importance
    C. should cover as many of the activities of the program as possible
    D. should be set in the light of assumptions about future funding

20. Assume that you have been assigned responsibility for coordinating various aspects of the case aide program in a community social services center.
    Which of the following administrative concepts would NOT be applicable to this assignment?

    A. Functional job analysis
    B. Peer group supervision
    C. Differential use of staff
    D. Systems design

21. Good administrative practice includes the use of outside consultants as effective technique in achieving agency objectives.
    However, the one of the following which would NOT be an appropriate role for the consultant is

    A. provision of technical or professional expertise not otherwise available in the agency
    B. administrative direction of a new program activity
    C. facilitating coordination and communication among agency staff
    D. objective measurement of the effectiveness of agency services

22. Of the following, the MOST common fault of recent research projects attempting to measure the effectiveness of social programs has been their

    A. questionable methodology
    B. inaccurate findings
    C. unrealistic expectations
    D. lack of objectivity

23. One of the most difficult tasks of supervision in a modern public agency is teaching workers to cope with the hostile reactions of clients.
    In order to help the disconcerted worker analyze and understand a client's hostile behavior, the supervisor should FIRST

    A. encourage the worker to identify with the client's frustrations and deprivations
    B. give the worker a chance to express and accept his feelings about the client
    C. ask the worker to review his knowledge of the client and his circumstances
    D. explain to the worker that the client's anger is not directed at the worker personally

24. Determination of the level of participation, or how much of the public should participate in a given project, is a vital step in community organization.
    In order to make this determination, the FIRST action that should be taken is to

    A. develop the participants
    B. fix the goals of the project
    C. evaluate community interest in the project
    D. enlist the cooperation of community leaders

25. The one of the following which would be the MOST critical factor for successful operation of a decentralized system of social programs and services is

    A. periodic review and evaluation of services delivered at the community level
    B. transfer of decision-making authority to the community level wherever feasible
    C. participation of indigenous non-professionals in service delivery
    D. formulation of quantitative plans for dealing with community problems wherever feasible

KEY (CORRECT ANSWERS)

1. A
2. A
3. C
4. C
5. B

6. D
7. A
8. A
9. B
10. B

11. A
12. C
13. D
14. A
15. B

16. D
17. B
18. C
19. D
20. B

21. B
22. C
23. B
24. B
25. B

EXAMINATION SECTION
TEST 1

DIRECTIONS: Each question or incomplete statement is followed by several suggested answers or completions. Select the one that BEST answers the question or completes the statement. *PRINT THE LETTER OF THE CORRECT ANSWER IN THE SPACE AT THE RIGHT.*

1. An interview is BEST conducted in private primarily because
    A. the person interviewed will tend to be less self-conscious
    B. the interviewer will be able to maintain his continuity of thought better
    C. it will insure that the interview is "off the record"
    D. people tend to "show off" before an audience

2. An interviewer can BEST establish a good relationship with the person being interviewed by
    A. assuming casual interest in the statements made by the person being interviewed
    B. taking the point of view of the person interviewed
    C. controlling the interview to a major extent
    D. showing a genuine interest in the person

3. An interviewer will be better able to understand the person interviewed and his problems if he recognizes that much of the person's behavior is due to motives
    A. which are deliberate
    B. of which he is unaware
    C. which are inexplicable
    D. which are kept under control

4. An interviewer's attention must be directed toward himself as well as toward the person interviewed.
   This statement means that the interviewer should
    A. keep in mind the extent to which his own prejudices may influence his judgment
    B. rationalize the statements made by the person interviewed
    C. gain the respect and confidence of the person interviewed
    D. avoid being too impersonal

5. More complete expression will be obtained from a person being interviewed if the interviewer can create the impression that
    A. the data secured will become part of a permanent record
    B. official information must be accurate in every detail
    C. it is the duty of the person interviewed to give accurate data
    D. the person interviewed is participating in a discussion of his own problems

6. The practice of asking leading questions should be avoided in an interview because the
   A. interviewer risks revealing his attitudes to the person being interviewed
   B. interviewer may be led to ignore the objective attitudes of the person interviewed
   C. answers may be unwarrantedly influenced
   D. person interviewed will resent the attempt to lead him and will be less cooperative

7. A good technique for the interviewer to use in an effort to secure reliable data and to reduce the possibility of misunderstanding is to
   A. use casual undirected conversation, enabling the person being interviewed to talk about himself, and thus secure the desired information
   B. adopt the procedure of using direct questions regularly
   C. extract the desired information from the person being interviewed by putting him on the defensive
   D. explain to the person being interviewed the information desired and the reason for needing it

8. You are interviewing a patient to determine whether she is eligible for medical assistance. Of the many questions that you have to ask her, some are routine questions that patients tend to answer willingly and easily. Other questions are more personal and some patients tend to resent being asked them and avoid answering them directly.
   For you to begin the interview with the more personal questions would be
   A. *desirable*, because the end of the interview will go smoothly and the patient will be left with a warm feeling
   B. *undesirable*, because the patient might not know the answers to the questions
   C. *desirable*, because you will be able to return to these questions later to verify the accuracy of the responses
   D. *undesirable*, because you might antagonize the patient before you have had a chance to establish rapport

9. While interviewing a patient about her family composition, the patient asks you whether you are married.
   Of the following, the MOST appropriate way for you to handle this situation is to
   A. answer the question briefly and redirect her back to the topic under discussion
   B. refrain from answering the question and proceed with the interview
   C. advise the patient that it is more important that she answer your questions than that you answer hers, and proceed with the interview
   D. promise the patient that you will answer her question later, in the hope that she will forget, and redirect her back to the topic under discussion

10. In response to a question about his employment history, a patient you are interviewing rambles and talks about unrelated matters.
    Of the following, the MOST appropriate course of action for you to take FIRST is to

A. ask questions to direct the patient back to his employment history
B. advise him to concentrate on your questions and not to discuss irrelevant information
C. ask him why he is resisting a discussion of his employment history
D. advise him that if you cannot get the information you need, he will not be eligible for medical assistance

11. Suppose that a person you are interviewing becomes angry at some of the questions you have asked, calls you meddlesome and nosy, and states that she will not answer those questions.
Of the following, which is the BEST action for you to take?
    A. Explain the reasons the questions are asked and the importance of the answers
    B. Inform the interviewee that you are only doing your job and advise her that she should answer your questions or leave the office
    C. Report to your supervisor what the interviewee called you and refuse to continue the interview
    D. End the interview and tell the interviewee she will not be serviced by your department

11.____

12. Suppose that during the course of an interview the interviewee demands in a very rude way that she be permitted to talk to your supervisor or someone in charge.
Which of the following is probably the BEST way to handle this situation?
    A. Inform your supervisor of the demand and ask her to speak to the interviewee
    B. Pay no attention to the demands of the interviewee and continue the interview
    C. Report to your supervisor and tell her to get another interviewer for this interviewee
    D. Tell her you are the one "in charge" and that she should talk to you

12.____

13. Of the following, the outcome of an interview by an aide depends MOST heavily on the
    A. personality of the interviewee
    B. personality of the aide
    C. subject matter of the questions asked
    D. interaction between aide and interviewee

13.____

14. Some patients being interviewed are primarily interested in making a favorable impression.
The aide should be aware of the fact that such patients are more likely than other patients to
    A. try to anticipate the answers the interviewer is looking for
    B. answer all questions openly and frankly
    C. try to assume the role of interviewer
    D. be anxious to get the interview over as quickly as possible

14.____

15. The type of interview which an aide usually conducts is substantially different from most interviewing situations in all of the following aspects EXCEPT the
    A. setting
    B. kinds of clients
    C. techniques employed
    D. kinds of problems

16. During an interview, an aide uses a "leading question."
    This type of question is so-called because it generally
    A. starts a series of questions about one topic
    B. suggests the answer which the aide wants
    C. forms the basis for a following "trick" question
    D. sets, at the beginning, the tone of the interview

17. Casework interviewing is always directed to the client and his situation. The one of the following which is the MOST accurate statement with respect to the proper focus of an interview is that the
    A. caseworker limits the client to concentration on objective data
    B. client is generally permitted to talk about facts and feelings with no direction from the caseworker
    C. main focus in casework interviews is on feelings rather than facts
    D. caseworker is responsible for helping the client focus on any material which seems to be related to his problems or difficulties

18. Assume that you are conducting a training program for the caseworkers under your supervision. At one of the sessions, you discuss the problem of interviewing a dull and stupid client who gives a slow and disconnected case history.
    The BEST of the following interviewing methods for you to recommend in such a case in order to ascertain facts is for the caseworker to
    A. ask the client leading questions requiring "yes" or "no" answers
    B. request the client to limit his narration to the essential facts so that the interview can be kept as brief as possible
    C. review the story with the client, patiently asking simple questions
    D. tell the client that unless he is more cooperative he cannot be helped to solve his problem

19. A recent development in casework interviewing procedure, known as multiple-client interviewing, consists of interviews of the entire family at the same time. However, this may not be an effective casework method in certain situations.
    Of the following, the situation in which the standard individual interview would be preferable is when
    A. family member derive consistent and major gratification from assisting each other in their destructive responses
    B. there is a crucial family conflict to which the members are reacting
    C. the family is overwhelmed by interpersonal anxieties which have not been explored
    D. the worker wants to determine the pattern of family interaction to further his diagnostic understanding

20. A follow-up interview was arranged for an applicant in order that he could furnish 20.____
certain requested evidence. At this follow-up interview, the applicant still fails
to furnish the necessary evidence.
It would be MOST advisable for you to
   A. advise the applicant that he is now considered ineligible
   B. ask the applicant how soon he can get the necessary evidence and set a date for another interview
   C. question the applicant carefully and thoroughly to determine if he has misrepresented or falsified any information
   D. set a date for another interview and tell the applicant to get the necessary evidence by that time

KEY (CORRECT ANSWERS)

1.	A	11.	A
2.	D	12.	A
3.	B	13.	D
4.	A	14.	A
5.	D	15.	C
6.	C	16.	B
7.	D	17.	D
8.	D	18.	C
9.	A	19.	A
10.	A	20.	B

TEST 2

DIRECTIONS: Each question or incomplete statement is followed by several suggested answers or completions. Select the one that BEST answers the question or completes the statement. *PRINT THE LETTER OF THE CORRECT ANSWER IN THE SPACE AT THE RIGHT.*

1. In interviewing, the practice of anticipating an applicant's answers to questions is generally
   A. *desirable*, because it is effective and economical when it is necessary to interview large numbers of applicants
   B. *desirable*, because many applicants have language difficulties
   C. *undesirable*, because it is the inalienable right of every person to answer as he sees fit
   D. *undesirable*, because applicants may tend to agree with the answer proposed by the interviewer even when the answer is not entirely correct

2. When an initial interview is being conducted, one way of starting is to explain the purpose of the interview to the applicant.
   The practice of starting the interview with such an explanation is generally
   A. *desirable*, because the applicant can then understand why the interview is necessary and what will be accomplished by it
   B. *desirable*, because it creates the rapport which is necessary to successful interviewing
   C. *undesirable*, because time will be saved by starting directly with the questions which must be asked
   D. *undesirable*, because the interviewer should have the choice of starting an interview in any manner he prefers

3. For you to use responses such as "That's interesting," "Uh-huh," and "Good" during an interview with a patient is
   A. *desirable*, because they indicate that the investigator is attentive
   B. *undesirable*, because they are meaningless to the patient
   C. *desirable*, because the investigator is not supposed to talk excessively
   D. *undesirable*, because they tend to encourage the patient to speak freely

4. During the course of a routine interview, the BEST tone of voice for an interviewer to use is
   A. authoritative
   B. uncertain
   C. formal
   D. conversational

5. It is recommended that interviews which inquire into the personal background of an individual should be held in private.
   The BEST reason for this practice is that privacy
   A. allows the individual to talk freely about the details of his background
   B. induces contemplative thought on the part of the interviewed individual
   C. prevents any interruptions by departmental personnel during the interview
   D. most closely resembles the atmosphere of the individual's personal life

6. Assume that you are interviewing a patient to determine whether he has any savings accounts.
   To obtain this information, the MOST effective way to phrase your question would be:
   A. "You don't have any savings, do you?"
   B. "At which bank do you have a savings account?"
   C. "Do you have a savings account?"
   D. "May I assume that you have a savings account?"

7. You are interviewing a patient who is not cooperating to the extent necessary to get all required information. Therefore, you decide to be more forceful in your approach.
   In this situation, such a course of action is
   A. *advisable*, because such a change in approach may help to increase the patient's participation
   B. *advisable*, because you will be using your authority more effectively
   C. *inadvisable*, because you will not be able to change this approach if it doesn't produce results
   D. *inadvisable*, because an aggressive approach generally reduces the validity of the interview

8. You have attempted to interview a patient on two separate occasions, and both attempts were unsuccessful. The patient has been totally uncooperative and you sense a personal hostility toward you.
   Of the following, the BEST way to handle this type of situation would be to
   A. speak to the patient in a courteous manner and ask him to explain exactly what he dislikes about you
   B. inform the patient that you will not allow personality conflicts to disrupt the interview
   C. make no further attempt to interview the patient and recommend that he be billed in full
   D. discuss the problem with your supervisor and suggest that another investigator be assigned to try to interview the patient

9. At the beginning of an interview, a patient with normal vision tells you that he is reluctant to discuss his finances. You realize that it will be necessary in this case to ask detailed questions about his net income.
   When you begin this line of questioning, of the following, the LEAST important aspect you should consider is your
   A. precise wording of the question   B. manner of questioning
   C. tone of voice   D. facial expressions

10. A caseworker under your supervision has been assigned the task of interviewing a man who is applying for foster home placement for his two children. The caseworker seeks your advice as to how to question this man, stating that she finds the applicant to be a timid and self-conscious person who seems torn between the necessity of having to answer the worker's questions truthfully and the effect he thinks his answers will have on his application.

Of the following, the BEST method for the caseworker to use in order to determine the essential facts in this case is to
- A. assure the applicant that he need not worry since the majority of applications for foster home placement are approved
- B. delay the applicant's narration of the facts important to the case until his embarrassment and fears have been overcome
- C. ignore the statements made by the applicant and obtain all the required information from his friends and relatives
- D. inform the applicant that all statements made by him will be verified and are subject to the law governing perjury

11. Assume that a worker is interviewing a boy in his assigned group in order to help him find a job.
At the BEGINNING of the interview, the worker should
    - A. suggest a possible job for the youth
    - B. refer the youth to an employment agency
    - C. discuss the youth's work history and skills with him
    - D. refer the youth to the manpower and career development agency

12. As part of the investigation to locate an absent father, you make a field visit to interview one of the father's friends. Before beginning the interview, you identify yourself to the friend and show him your official identification.
For you to do this is, generally,
    - A. *good practice*, because the friend will have proof that you are authorized to make such confidential investigations
    - B. *poor practice*, because the friend may not answer your questions when he knows why you are interviewing him
    - C. *good practice*, because your supervisor can confirm from the friend that you actually made the interview
    - D. *poor practice*, because the friend may warn the absent father that your agency is looking for him

13. You are interviewing a client in his home as part of your investigation of an anonymous complaint that he has been receiving Medicaid fraudulently.
During the interview, the client frequently interrupts your questions to discuss the hardships of his life and the bitterness he feels about his medical condition.
Of the following, the BEST way for you to deal with these discussions is to
    - A. cut them off abruptly, since the client is probably just trying to avoid answering your questions
    - B. listen patiently, since these discussions may be helpful to the client and may give you information for your investigation
    - C. remind the client that you are investigating a complaint against him and he must answer directly
    - D. seek to gain the client's confidence by discussing any personal or medical problems which you yourself may have

14. While interviewing an absent father to determine his ability to pay child support, you realize that his answers to some of your questions contradict his answers to other questions.
Of the following, the BEST way for you to try to get accurate information from the father is to
   A. confront him with his contradictory answers and demand an explanation from him
   B. use your best judgment as to which of his answers are accurate and question him accordingly
   C. tell him that he has misunderstood your questions and that he must clarify his answers
   D. ask him the same questions in different words and follow up his answer with related questions

14.____

15. Assume that an applicant, obviously under a great deal of stress, talks continuously and rambles, making it difficult for you to determine the exact problem and her need.
In order to make the interview more successful, it would be BEST for you to
   A. interrupt the applicant and ask her specific questions in order to get the information you need
   B. tell the applicant that her rambling may be a basic cause of her problem
   C. let the applicant continue talking as long as she wishes
   D. ask the applicant to get to the point because other people are waiting for you

15.____

16. A worker must be able to interview clients all day and still be able to listen and maintain interest.
Of the following, it is MOST important for you to show interest in the client because, if you appear interested,
   A. the client is more likely to appreciate your professional status
   B. the client is more likely to disclose a greater amount of information
   C. the client is less likely to tell lie
   D. you are more likely to gain your supervisor's approval

16.____

17. When you are interviewing clients, it is important to notice and record how they say what they say—angrily, nervously, or with "body English"—because these signs may
   A. tell you that the client's words are the opposite of what the client feels and you may need to dig to find out what those feeling are
   B. be the prelude to violent behavior which no aide is prepared to handle
   C. show that the client does not really deserve serious consideration
   D. be important later should you be asked to defend what you did for the client

17.____

18. The patient you are interviewing is reticent and guarded in responding to your questions. He is not providing the information needed to complete his application for medical assistance.
In this situation, the one of the following which is the MOST appropriate course of action for you to take FIRST is to

18.____

A. end the interview and ask him to contact you when he is ready to answer your questions
B. advise the patient that you cannot end the interview until he has provided all the information you need to complete the application
C. emphasize to the patient the importance of the questions and the need to answer them in order to complete the application
D. advise the patient that if he answers your questions the interview will be easier for both of you

19. At the end of an interview with a patient, he describes a problem he is having with his teenage son, who is often truant and may be using narcotics. The patient asks you for advice in handling his son.
Of the following, the MOST appropriate action for you to take is to
    A. make an appointment to see the patient and his son together
    B. give the patient a list of drug counseling programs to which he may refer his son
    C. suggest to the patient that his immediate concern should be his own hospitalization rather than his son's problem
    D. tell the patient that you are not qualified to assist him but will attempt to find out who can

19.____

20. A MOST appropriate condition in the use of direct questions to obtain personal data in an interview is that, whenever possible,
    A. the direct questions be used only as a means of encouraging the person interviewed to talk about himself
    B. provision be made for recording the information
    C. the direct questions be used only after all other methods have failed
    D. the person being interviewed understands the reason for requesting the information

20.____

KEY (CORRECT ANSWERS)

1.	D	11.	C
2.	A	12.	A
3.	A	13.	B
4.	D	14.	D
5.	A	15.	A
6.	B	16.	B
7.	A	17.	A
8.	D	18.	C
9.	A	19.	D
10.	B	20.	D

READING COMPREHENSION
UNDERSTANDING AND INTERPRETING WRITTEN MATERIAL
EXAMINATION SECTION
TEST 1

DIRECTIONS: Each question or incomplete statement is followed by several suggested answers or completions. Select the one that BEST answers the question or completes the statement. *PRINT THE LETTER OF THE CORRECT ANSWER IN THE SPACE AT THE RIGHT.*

Questions 1-4.

DIRECTIONS: Questions 1 through 4 are to be answered SOLELY on the basis of the information in the following paragraphs.

    Some authorities have questioned whether the term *culture of poverty* should be used since *culture* means a design for living which is passed down from generation to generation. The culture of poverty is, however, a very useful concept if it is used with care, with recognition that poverty is a subculture, and with avoidance of the *cookie-cutter* approached. With regard to the individual, the cookie-cutter view assumes that all individuals in a culture turn out exactly alike, as if they were so many cookies. It overlooks the fact that, at least in our urban society, every individual is a member of more than one subculture; and which subculture most strongly influences his response in a given situation depends on the interaction of a great many factors, including his individual make-up and history, the specifics of the various subcultures to which he belongs, and the specifics of the given situation. It is always important to avoid the cookie-cutter view of culture, with regard to the individual and to the culture or subculture involved.

    With regard to the culture as a whole, the cookie-cutter concept again assumes homogeneity and consistency. It forgets that within any one culture or subculture there are conflicts and contradictions, and that at any given moment an individual may have to choose, consciously, between conflicting values or patterns. Also, most individuals, in varying degrees, have a dual set of values—those by which they live and those they cherish as best. This point has been made and documented repeatedly about the culture of poverty.

1. The *cookie-cutter* approach assumes that
    A. members of the same *culture* are all alike
    B. *culture* stays the same from generation to generation
    C. the term *culture* should not be applied to groups who are poor
    D. there are value conflicts within most *cultures*

    1.____

2. According to the above passage, every person in our cities
    A. is involved in the conflicts of urban culture
    B. recognizes that poverty is a subculture
    C. lives by those values too which he is exposed
    D. belongs to more than one subculture

    2.____

3. The above passage emphasizes that a culture is likely to contain within it 3.____
   A. one dominant set of values
   B. a number of contradictions
   C. one subculture to which everyone belongs
   D. members who are exactly alike

4. According to the above passage, individuals are sometimes forced to choose BETWEEN 4.____
   A. cultures
   B. subcultures
   C. different sets of values
   D. a new culture and an old culture

Questions 5-8.

DIRECTIONS: Questions 5 through 8 are to be answered SOLELY on the basis of the following passage.

There are approximately 33 million poor people in the United States; 14.3 million of them are children, 5.3 million are old people, and the remainder are in other categories. Altogether, 6.5 million families live in poverty because the head of household cannot work; they are either too old or too sick or too severely handicapped, or they are widowed or deserted mothers of young children. There are the working poor: the low-paid workers, the workers in seasonal industries, and soldiers with no additional income who are heads of families. There are the underemployed: those who would like full-time jobs but cannot find them, those employees who would like year-round work but lack of opportunity, and those who are employed below their level of training. There are the non-working poor: the older men and women with small retirement incomes and those with no income, the disabled, the physically and mentally handicapped, and the chronically sick.

5. According to the above passage, approximately what percent of the poor people in the United States are children? 5.____
   A. 33   B. 16   C. 20   D. 44

6. According to the above passage, people who work in seasonal industries are LIKELY to be classified as 6.____
   A. working poor
   B. underemployed
   C. non-working poor
   D. low-paid workers

7. According to the above passage, the category of non-working poor includes people who 7.____
   A. receive unemployment insurance
   B. cannot find full-time work
   C. are disabled or mentally handicapped
   D. are soldiers with wives and children

8. According to the above passage, among the underemployed are those who 8.____
   A. can find only part-time work
   B. are looking for their first jobs
   C. are inadequately trained
   D. depend on insufficient retirement incomes

Questions 9-13.

DIRECTIONS: Read the Inter-office Memo below. Then, answer Questions 9 through 13 SOLELY on the basis of the memo.

INTER-OFFICE MEMORANDUM

To: Alma Robinson, Human Resources Aide

From: Frank Shields, Social Worker

I would like to have you help Mr. Edward Tunney, who is trying to raise his two children by himself. He needs to learn to improve the physical care of his children and especially of his daughter Helen, age 9. She is avoided and ridiculed at school because her hair is uncombed, her teeth not properly cleaned, her clothing torn, wrinkled and dirty, as well as shabby and poorly fitted. The teachers and school officials have contacted the Department and the social worker for two years about Helen. She is not able to make friends because of these problems. I have talked to Mr. Tunney about improvements for the child's clothing, hair, and hygiene. He tends to deny these things are problems, but is cooperative, and a second person showing him the importance of better physical care for Helen would be helpful.

Perhaps you could teach Helen how to fix her own hair. She has all the materials. I would also like you to form your own opinion of the sanitary conditions in the home and how they could be improved.

Mr. Tunney is expecting your visit and is willing to talk with you about ways he can help with these problems.

9. In the above memorandum, the Human Resources Aide is being asked to help Mr. Tunney to
   A. improve the learning habits of his children
   B. enable his children to make friends at school
   C. take responsibility for the upbringing of his children
   D. give attention to the grooming and cleanliness of his children

10. This case was brought to the attention of the social worker by
    A. government officials
    B. teachers and school officials
    C. the Department
    D. Mr. Tunney

11. In general, Mr. Tunney's attitude with regard to his children could BEST be described as
    A. interested in correcting the obvious problem, but unable to do so alone
    B. unwilling to follow the advice of those who are trying to help
    C. concerned but unaware of the seriousness of these problems
    D. interested in helping them, but afraid of taking the advice of the social worker

12. Which of the following actions has NOT been suggested as a possible step for the Human Resource Aide to take? 12.____
    A. Help Helen to learn to care for herself by teaching her grooming skills
    B Determine was of improvement gathered on a home visit
    C. Discuss her own views on Helen's problems with school officials
    D. Ask Mr. Tunney in what ways he believes the physical care may be improved

13. According to the above memo, the Human Resources Aide is ESPECIALLY being asked to observe and form her own opinions about 13.____
    A. the relationship between Mr. Tunney and the school officials
    B. Helen's attitude toward her classmates and teacher
    C. the sanitary conditions in the home
    D. the reasons Mr. Tunney is not cooperative with the agency

Questions 14-16.

DIRECTIONS: Questions 14 through 16 are to be answered SOLELY on the basis of the following paragraph.

In social work, professional responsibility and accountability extend to a larger segment of the general community than is true of the older professions which have more limited and more specialized areas of community responsibility and public trust. Advances in knowledge about both the nature of human institutions and the nature of the individual have placed social work in the center of a vast complex of interrelationships. The situations that come to the attention of the social worker, whatever his functions, may be the circumstances of an individual client or of a group or of a community which may or may not be socially sanctioned, and the proposed remedy may be considered desirable or questionable. When there is agreement between the client group and the community on the nature of the problem and on the validity of the proposed remedy, such agreement may lead to the establishment of social institutions. Complication arise when the client or client group, or the community, does not accept the need for change or is not in agreement with the social worker about the direction it should take. The social worker has the obligation to pursue his objective regardless of the difficulties. Even if social work, as it is practiced today, were to achieve the degree of acceptance afforded the older professions, it would still find itself, with every new development, holding unorthodox and not very respectful views on many aspects of personal and social relationships.

14. The MOST accurate of the following statements about the relationship between social work and the other professions is: 14.____
    A. Advances in knowledge have placed social work in a central position among the professions
    B. Although younger, social work has become basic to the older professions in their responsibility and accountability in the community
    C. It is the responsibility of social workers to hold unorthodox views on social relationships
    D. The areas of responsibility of social work within the community are more extensive than those of the older professions

15. When, because of an existing problem, a social worker has advocated a change in a social institution which has been opposed by the community, the social worker should
    A. attempt to surmount the opposition, continuing to seek to reach his objective
    B. change his position to gain the support of the community
    C. review the position that he has taken to see whether he cannot revise his objective to the point where it may gain community support
    D. work to achieve for his profession the degree of acceptance which is afforded the older professions

16. Of the following, the BEST title for the above paragraph is
    A. DANGERS OF SOCIAL RESPONSIBILITY
    B. SOCIAL WORK AND THE OLDER PROFESSION COMPARED
    C. SOCIAL WORKERS' RESPONSIBILITY IN SOCIAL CHANGE
    D. UNORTHODOX SOCIAL WORK

Questions 17-19.

DIRECTIONS: Questions 17 through 19 are to be answered SOLELY on the basis of the following paragraphs.

Toward the end of the 19th century, as social work principles and theories took form, areas of conflict between the responsibility of the social worker to the client group and to the status quo of social and economic institutions became highlighted. The lay public's attitude toward the individual poor was one of emphasis on betterment through the development of the individual's capacity for self-maintenance. They hoped to maintain this end both by helping the client to rely on his unused capacities for self-help and by facilitating is access to what were assumed to be the natural sources of help family, relatives, churches, and other charitable associations. Professional social workers were fast becoming aware of the need for social reform. They perceived that traditional methods of help were largely inadequate to cope with the factors that were creating poverty and maladjustment for a large number of the population faster than the charity societies could relieve such problems through individual effort. The critical view, held by social workers, of the character of many social institutions was not shared by other groups in the community who had not reached the same point of awareness about the deficiencies in the functioning of these institutions. Thus, the views of the social worker were beginning to differ, sometimes radically, from the basic views of large sections of the population.

17. The social workers of the late 19th century found themselves in conflict with the status quo CHIEFLY because they
    A. had become professionalized through the development of a body of theory and principles
    B. became aware that many social ills could not be cured through existing institutions
    C. felt that traditional methods of helping the poor must be expanded regardless of the cost to the public
    D. believed that the right of the individual to be self-determining should be emphasized

18. It was becoming apparent, by the end of the 19th century, that in relation to the needs of the poor, existing social institutions
    A. did not sufficiently emphasize the ability of the poor to utilize their natural sources of help
    B. were using the proper methods of helping the poor, but were hindered by the work of social workers who had broken with tradition
    C. were no longer capable of meeting the needs of the poor because the causes of poverty had changed
    D. were capable of meeting the needs of the poor, but needed more financial aid from the general public since the number of people in need had increased

18.____

19. Social workers at the end of the 19th century may be PROPERLY classified as
    A. growing in awareness that many social ills could be alleviated through social reform
    B. very perceptive individuals who realized that traditional methods of help were humiliating to the poor
    C. strong advocates of expanding the existing traditional sources of relief
    D. too radical because they favored easing life for the poor at the expense of increased taxation to the public at large

19.____

Questions 20-24.

DIRECTIONS: Questions 20 through 24 are to be answered SOLELY on the basis of the following paragraphs.

With the generation gap yawning before us, it is well to remember that 20 years ago teenagers produced a larger proportion of unwedlock births than today, and that the illegitimacy rate among teenagers is lower than among women in their twenties and thirties. In addition, the illegitimacy rate has risen less among teenagers than among older women.

It is helpful to note the difference between illegitimacy rate and illegitimacy ratio. The ratio is the number of illegitimate babies per 1,000 live births. The rate is the number of illegitimate births per 1,000 unmarried women of childbearing age. The ratio talks about babies; the rate talks about mothers. The ratio is useful for planning services, but worse than useless for considering trends since it depends on the age and marital composition of the population, illegitimacy rate, and the fertility of married women. For example, the ratio among girls under 18 is bound to be high in comparison with older women since few are married mothers. However, the illegitimacy rate is relatively low.

20. Of the following, the MOST suitable title for the above passage would be
    A. THE GENERATION GAP
    B. MORAL STANDARDS AND TEENAGE ILLEGITIMACY RATIO
    C. A COMPARISON OF ILLEGITIMACY RATE AND ILLEGITIMACY RATIO
    D. CAUSES OF HIGH ILLEGITIMACY RATES

20.____

21. According to the above passage, which of the following statements is CORRECT?
    The illegitimacy
    A. rate has fallen among women in their thirties
    B. ratio is the number of illegitimate births per 1,000 unmarried women of childbearing age
    C. ratio is partially dependent on the illegitimacy rate
    D. rate is more useful than the ratio for planning services

22. According to the above passage, of the following age groups, the illegitimacy ratio would be expected to be HIGHEST in comparison with the other groups for the group aged
    A. 17   B. 21   C. 25   D. 29

23. According to the above passage, of the following age groups, the illegitimacy rate would be expected to be LOWEST in comparison with the other groups for the group aged
    A. 17   B. 21   C. 25   D. 29

24. As used in the above passage, the underlined word *composition* means MOST NEARLY
    A. essay   B. makeup   C. security   D. happiness

25. A document was published by a public agency and distributed for discussion. The document contained data showing trends in the level of reading among freshmen college students and suggested that the high schools were not investing enough effort in overcoming retardation. It compared the costs of intensifying reading instruction in the secondary schools as compared to costs in colleges for such instruction.
    According to the above statement, it is REASONABLE to conclude that
    A. the document proposed new programs
    B. the college students read better than high school students
    C. some college students need remedial reading
    D. the study was done by a consultant

KEY (CORRECT ANSWERS)

1.	A	11.	C
2.	D	12.	C
3.	B	13.	C
4.	C	14.	D
5.	D	15.	A
6.	A	16.	C
7.	C	17.	B
8.	A	18.	C
9.	D	19.	A
10.	B	20.	C

21. C
22. A
23. A
24. B
25. C

TEST 2

DIRECTIONS: Each question or incomplete statement is followed by several suggested answers or completions. Select the one that BEST answers the question or completes the statement. *PRINT THE LETTER OF THE CORRECT ANSWER IN THE SPACE AT THE RIGHT.*

Questions 1-4.

DIRECTIONS: Questions 1 through 4 are to be answered SOLELY on the basis of the following paragraph.

    Form W-280 provides a uniform standard for estimating family expenses and is used as a basis for determining eligibility for the care of children at public expense. The extent to which legally responsible relatives can pay for the care of a child must be computed. The minimum amount of the payment required from legally responsible relatives shall be 50% of the budget surplus as computed on Form W-281, plus any governmental benefits, such as OASDI benefits, or Railroad Retirement benefits being paid to a family member for the child receiving care or services. Because of the kinds and quantities of services included in the budget schedule (W-280) and because only 50% of the budget surplus is required as payment, no allowances for special needs are made, except for verified payments into civil service pension funds, amounts paid to a garnishee, or amounts paid to another agency for the care of other relatives for whom the relative is legally responsible, or for other such expenses if approval has been granted after Form W-278 has been submitted. In determining the income of the legally responsible relative, income from wages, self-employment, unemployment insurance benefits, and any such portion of governmental benefits as is not specifically designated for children already receiving care is to be included. Should 50% of the family's surplus meet the child care expenses, the case shall not be processed. Form W-279, an agreement to support, shall be signed by the legally responsible relative when 50% of the surplus is $1.00 or more a week.

1. A family is required to sign an agreement to support
   A. whenever they are legally responsible for the support of the child under care
   B. before any care at public expense is given to the child
   C. when their income surplus is at least $2.00/week
   D. when 50% of their income surplus meets the full needs of the child

1.____

2. The reason for allowing a family to deduct only certain specified expenses when computing the amount they are able to contribute to the support of a child being cared for at public expense is that the family
   A. should not be permitted to have a higher standard of living than the child being cared for
   B. the budget schedule is sufficiently generous and includes an allowance for other unusual expenses
   C. may not be able to verify their extraordinary expenses
   D. may meet other unusual expenses from the remainder of their surplus

2.____

3. Mrs. B. wishes to have her daughter, Mary, cared for at public expense. Her income includes her wages and OASDI benefits of $250 a month, of which $50 a month is paid for Mary and $50 a month for another minor member of the family who is already being cared for at public expense.
In order to determine the amount of Mrs. B.'s budget surplus, it is necessary to consider as income her wages and
   A. $50 of OASDI received for Mary
   B. $150 of the OASDI benefits
   C. $200 of the OASDI benefits
   D. $200 of the OASDI benefits if she is legally responsible for the care of the other child in placement

4. In order to determine a family's ability to contribute to the support of a child, the worker should
   A. have the legally responsible member sign Form W-279 agreeing to support the child, and then compute the family surplus on W-281 in accordance with public assistance standards
   B. compute the family's income in accordance with the allowance included on Form W-280 and the expenses included on Form W-279 and have Form W-279 signed if necessary
   C. use Form W-278 to work out a budget schedule for the family and compute their surplus on W-281 and then have them sign W-279 if necessary
   D. compute income and expenses on Form W-281, based on Form W-280, and have Form W-279 signed if necessary

Questions 5-10.

DIRECTIONS: Questions 5 through 10 are to be answered SOLELY on the basis of the following passage.

Too often in the past, society has accepted the existing social welfare programs, preferring to tinker with refinements when fundamental reform was in order. It has been a demeaning degrading welfare system in which the instrument of government was wrongfully and ineptly used. It has been a system which has only alienated those forced to benefit from it and demoralized those who had to administer it at the level where the pain was clearly visible.

There is a need to put this nation on a course in which cash benefits, providing a basic level of support, are conferred in such a way as to intrude as little as possible into privacy and self-respect. It is difficult to define a basic level of support, no matter how high or low it might be set. In the end, however, the design is not determined so much by how much is truly adequate for a family to meet all of its needs, but by the resources available to carry out the promise. That may be a harsh fact of life but it is also just that—a fact of life

5. Of the following, the MOST suitable title for the above passage would be
   A. THE NEED FOR GOVERNMENT CONTROL OF WELFARE
   B. DETERMINING THE BASIC LEVEL OF SUPPORT
   C. THE NEED FOR WELFARE REFORM
   D. THE ELIMINATION OF WELFARE PROGRAMS

6. In the above passage, the author's GREATEST criticism of the welfare system is that it is too
   A. disrespectful of recipients
   B. expensive to administer
   C. limited by regulations
   D. widespread in application

7. According to the above passage, the BASIC level of support is actually determined by
   A. how much is required for a family to meet all of its needs
   B. the age of the recipients
   C. how difficult it is to administer the program
   D. the economic resources of the nation

8. In the above passage, the author does NOT argue for
   A. a work incentive system
   B. a basic level of support
   C. cash benefits
   D. the privacy of recipients

9. As used in the above passage, the underlined word demeaning means MOST NEARLY
   A. ineffective
   B. expensive
   C. overburdened
   D. humiliating

10. As used in the above passage, the underlined word ineptly means MOST NEARLY
    A. foolishly
    B. unsuccessfully
    C. unskillfully
    D. unhappily

Questions 11-14.

DIRECTIONS: Questions 11 through 14 are to be answered SOLELY on the basis of the following paragraph.

The employment rate, which counts those unemployed in the sense that they are actively looking for work and unable to find it, gives a relatively superficial index of economic conditions in a community. A better index is the subemployment rate which includes the unemployment rate and also includes those working part-time while they are trying to get full-time work; those heads of households under 65 years of age who earn less than $240 per week working full-time, and those individuals under 65 who are not heads of households and earn less than $224 per week in a full-time job; and an estimate of the males *not counted*, which is a very real concern in ghetto areas.

11. Of the following, the MOST suitable title for the above paragraph would be
    A. EMPLOYMENT IN THE UNITED STATES
    B. PART-TIME WORKERS AND THE ECONOMY
    C. THE LABOR MARKET AND THE COMMUNITY
    D. TWO INDICATORS OF ECONOMIC CONDITIONS

12. On the basis of the above paragraph, which of the following statements is CORRECT?   12.____
    A. The unemployment rate includes everyone who is not fully employed.
    B. The subemployment rate is higher than the unemployment rate.
    C. The unemployment rate gives a more complete picture of the economic situation than the subemployment rate.
    D. The subemployment rate indicates how many part-time workers are dissatisfied with the number of hours they work per week.

13. As used in the above paragraph, the underlined word superficial means MOST NEARLY   13.____
    A. exaggerated   B. official   C. surface   D. current

14. According to the above paragraph, which of the following is included in the subemployment rate?   14.____
    A. Everyone who is unemployed
    B. All part-time workers
    C. Everyone under 65 who earns less than $220 per week in a full-time job
    D. All heads of households who earn less than $240 per week in a full-time job

Questions 15-16.

DIRECTIONS: Questions 15 and 16 are to be answered SOLELY on the basis of the following paragraphs.

The city's economy has its own dynamics, and there is only so much the government can do to shape it. But that margin is critically important. If the city uses its points of leverage, it can generate a large number of jobs—and good jobs, jobs that lead to advancement.

As a major employer itself, the city can upgrade the jobs it offers and greatly improve its services to the public if it does so. Since highly skilled professionals will always be in short supply, the city must train more paraprofessionals to take over routine tasks. Equally important, it must provide them with a realistic job ladder so they can move on up—nurse's aide to certified nurse, for example, teacher's aide to teacher. The training programs for such upgrading will require a substantial public investment but the cost-benefit return should be excellent.

As a major purchaser of goods and services, the city can stimulate business enterprise in the ghetto. The growth of Blacks and Puerto Rican firms will produce more local jobs; it will also create the kind of managerial talent the ghetto needs.

New kinds of enterprise can be set up. In housing, for example, there is a huge backlog of rehabilitation work to be done and a large pool of unskilled manpower to be trained for it. Corporations can be formed to take over tenements, remodel, and operate them, as in the Brownsville Home Maintenance Program. Grocery cooperatives to bring food prices down are another possibility.

15. According to the above paragraphs, the city is the major employer and by using its capacity it can
    A. assist unskilled people with talent to move up on the job ladder
    B. create private enterprises that will renew all areas of the city in need of renewal
    C. eliminate poverty in the ghetto areas by selective purchase of goods and services
    D. have no influence on the economy of the city

15.____

16. According to the above paragraph, one may REASONABLY conclude that
    A. the city has no power to influence the job market
    B. a byproduct of strategic purchasing and employment and training practices can be the rehabilitation of housing and the lowering of food prices
    C. highly skilled professions, which are now in short supply, will no longer be needed after paraprofessionals are trained to take over routine jobs
    D. the city's major objective is to bring down food prices

16.____

Questions 17-21.

DIRECTIONS: Questions 17 through 21 are to be answered SOLELY on the basis of the following paragraphs.
For each question, there are two statements.
Based on the information in the paragraphs, mark your answer:
A. If only statement is correct;
B. If only statement 2 is correct;
C. If both statements are correct;
D. if the excerpt do not contain sufficient evidence for concluding whether either or both statements are correct.

Upstate, 35% of the AFDC families lived in districts suburban to New York City, 43% in upstate urban districts, and 22% in the rest of upstate. Among white families, 28% resided in suburban districts, 40% in upstate urban districts, and 32% in the rest of upstate. Among non-white families, 43% lived in suburban districts, 47% in upstate urban districts, and 10% in the rest of upstate.

Upstate, 78.7% of the AFDC families resided in SMSA (Standard Metropolitan Statistical Area) counties, including 68.7% of the whites and 90.4% of the non-whites. In Buffalo, 83.3% of the families were non-white; in Rochester, 57.9% were non-whites; in cities of 100,000 to 250,000 (Albany, Syracuse, and Utica), 55.2% were white; and the rest of the upstate urban counties, 86.5% were white.

The two most frequent underlying reasons for a family requiring AFDC were desertion of the father (31.3% of the cases) and *father not married to mother* (30.%). Desertions were proportionately highest among Puerto Rican families (38.6%), compared with 29.4% for Blacks and 23.6% for white families. Unmarried mothers comprised 39.4% of the Black cases, compared with 26.6% for Puerto Ricans and 14.8% for white cases.

White families had substantially higher proportions in the separated and divorce categories than non-whites. When the deserted, separated, and divorced categories are combined, marital breakdown occurred in 59% of the white AFDC families, compared with 52.3% for Puerto Ricans and 44.4% for Blacks.

Substantial ethnic differences existed in the proportions of incapacitated fathers; overall, the rate was 7.5%, but among white families the rate was 14.8%, compared with 9.4% for Puerto Ricans and only 3.0% for Blacks. Families where the father was deceased comprised 5.9% of the AFDC cases.

In New York City, desertion rates (35.3% of all cases) were substantially higher than upstate (18.9%), particularly among white families, as ethnic differences in New York City diminished considerably. Unmarried mother rates closely paralleled the statewide figures.

Incapacity of the father occurred more frequently among white families upstate (17.5%) than among white families in New York City (104%). Deceased fathers were proportionately highest among the New York City Black and Puerto Rican caseload, possibly reflecting fewer remarriage and employment opportunities among these groups in the event of the death of the father.

17. 1. The most frequent underlying reason for a family requiring AFDC was *father not married to mother*.
    2. Three-fourths of New York State's AFDC families lived in New York City.

    17.____

18. 1. There were more cases of desertion among AFDC cases upstate than there were of incapacity of the father among white AFDC families upstate.
    2. There was a higher percentage of marital breakdowns among white AFDC families compared to Puerto Rican for Black families.

    18.____

19. 1. Desertion of the father accounted for more AFDC cases than all other reasons combined.
    2. The proportion of incapacitated fathers in Puerto Rican families was higher than the overall rate of incapacitated fathers.

    19.____

20. 1. Non-white families had substantially higher proportions in the divorced and separated categories than white families.
    2. Among AFDC families in New York State, there were more Puerto Ricans than Blacks in the combined deserted, separated, and divorced categories

    20.____

21. 1. In New York City, there was a higher percentage of unmarried mothers among Puerto Rican AFDC families than among white cases.
    2. Among white families, desertion rates were considerably higher upstate than in New York City.

    21.____

Questions 22-25.

DIRECTIONS: Questions 22 through 25 are to be answered SOLELY on the basis of the information in the following paragraph.

The question of what material is relevant is not as simple as it might seem. Frequently, material which seems irrelevant to the inexperienced has, because of the common tendency to disguise and distort and misplace one's feelings, considerable significance. It may be necessary to let the client *ramble on* for a while in order to clear the decks, as it were, so that he may get down to things that really are on his mind. On the other hand, with an already disturbed person, it may be important for the interviewer to know when to discourage further elaboration of upsetting material. This is especially the case where the worker would be unable to do anything about it. An inexperienced interviewer might, for instance, be intrigued with the bizarre elaboration of material that the psychotic produces, but further elaboration of this might encourage the client in his instability. A too random discussion may indicate that the interviewee is not certain in what areas the interviewer is prepared to help him, and he may be seeking some direction. Or again, satisfying though it may be for the interviewer to have the interviewee tell him intimate details, such revelations sometimes need to be checked or encouraged only in small doses. An interviewee who has *talked too much* often reveals subsequent anxiety. This is illustrated by the fact that frequently after a *confessional* interview, the interviewee surprises the interviewer by being withdrawn, inarticulate, or hostile, or by breaking the next appointment.

22. Sometimes a client may reveal certain personal information to an interviewer and subsequently may feel anxious about this revelation.
    If, during an interview, a client begins to discuss very personal matters, it would be BEST to
    A. tell the client, in no uncertain terms, that you're not interested in personal details
    B. ignore the client at this point
    C. encourage the client to elaborate further on the details
    D. inform the client that the information seems to be very personal

23. The author indicates that clients with severe psychological disturbances pose an especially difficult problem for the inexperienced interviewer.
    The DIFFICULTY lies in the possibility of the client
    A. becoming physically violent and harming the interviewer
    B. rambling on for a while
    C. revealing irrelevant details which may be followed by cancelled appointments
    D. reverting to an unstable state as a result of interview material

24. An interviewer should be constantly alert to the possibility of obtaining clues from the client as to the problem areas.
    According to the above passage, a client who discusses topics at random may be
    A. unsure of what problems the interviewer can provide help
    B. reluctant to discuss intimate details
    C. trying to impress the interviewer with his knowledge
    D. deciding what relevant material to elaborate on

25. The evaluation of a client's responses may reveal substantial information that may aid the interviewer in assessing the problem areas that are of concern to the client. Responses that seemed irrelevant at the time of the interview may be of significance because
    A. considerable significance is attached to all irrelevant material
    B. emotional feelings are frequently masked
    C. an initial rambling on is often a prelude to what is actually bothering the client
    D. disturbed clients often reveal subsequent anxiety

25.____

KEY (CORRECT ANSWERS)

1.	C	11.	D
2.	D	12.	B
3.	B	13.	C
4.	D	14.	C
5.	C	15.	A
6.	A	16.	B
7.	D	17.	D
8.	A	18.	C
9.	D	19.	B
10.	C	20.	D

21.	A
22.	D
23.	D
24.	A
25.	B

ARITHMETICAL REASONING
EXAMINATION SECTION
TEST 1

DIRECTIONS: Each question or incomplete statement is followed by several suggested answers or completions. Select the one that BEST answers the question or completes the statement. *PRINT THE LETTER OF THE CORRECT ANSWER IN THE SPACE AT THE RIGHT.*

1. On January 1, a family was receiving supplementary monthly public assistance of $280 for food, $240 for rent, and $140 for other necessities. In the spring, their rent rose by 10%, and their rent allotment was adjusted accordingly. In the summer, due to the death of a family member, their allotments for food and other necessities were reduced by 1/7.
   Their monthly allowance check in the fall should be
   A. $623   B. $644   C. $664   D. $684

2. Twice a month, a certain family receives a $340 general allowance for rent, food, and clothing expense. In addition, the family receives a specific supplementary allotment for utilities of $384 a year, which is added to their semi-monthly check.
   If the general allowance alone is reduced by 5%, what will be the TOTAL amount of their next semi-monthly check?
   A. $323   B. $339   C. $340   D. $355

3. If each supervising clerk in a certain unit sees an average of 9 clients in a 7-hour day and there are 15 supervising clerks in the unit, APPROXIMATELY how many clients will be seen in a 35-hour week?
   A. 315   B. 405   C. 675   D. 945

4. In one day, an aide receives 18 inquiries by phone and 27 inquiries in person. What percentage of the inquiries received that day were by phone?
   A. 33%   B. 40%   C. 45%   D. 60%

5. If the weekly paychecks for 5 employees are $258.64, $325.48, $287.50, and $313.12, then the combined weekly income for the 5 employee is
   A. $1,455.68   B. $1,456.08   C. $1,462.68   D. $1,474.08

6. Suppose that there are 17 aides working in an office where many community complaints are received by telephone. In one ten-day period, 4,250 calls were received.
   If the same number of calls were received each day and the aides divided the work load equally, about how many calls did each aide respond to daily?
   A. 25   B. 35   C. 75   D. 250

7. Suppose that an assignment was divided among 5 aides.
If the first aide spent 67 hours on the assignment, the second aide spent 95 hours, the third aide spent 52 hours, the fourth aide spent 78 hours, and the fifth aide spent 103 hours, what was the AVERAGE amount of time spent by each aide on the assignment? _____ hours.
A. 71   B. 75   C. 79   D. 83

7._____

8. If there are 240 employees in a center and 1/3 are absent on the day of a bad snowstorm, how many employees were at work in the center on that day?
A. 80   B. 120   C. 160   D. 200

8._____

9. Suppose that an aide takes 25 minutes to prepare a letter to a client.
If the aide is assigned to prepare 9 letters on a certain day, how much time should be set aside for this task? _____ hours.
A. 3¾   B. 4¼   C. 4¾   D. 5¼

9._____

10. Suppose that a certain center uses both Form A and Form B in the course of its daily work and that Form A is used 4 times as often as Form B.
If the total number of both forms used in one week is 750, how many times was Form A used?
A. 100   B. 200   C. 400   D. 600

10._____

11. Suppose a center has a budget of $2,185.40 from which 8 desks costing $156.10 apiece must be bought.
How many additional desks can be ordered from this budget after the 8 desks have been purchased?
A. 4   B. 6   C. 9   D. 14

11._____

12. When researching a particular case, a team of 16 aides was asked to check through 234 folders to obtain the necessary information.
If half the aides worked twice as fast as the other half, and the slow group checked through 12 folders each hour, about how long would it take to complete the assignment? _____ hours.
A. 4¼   B. 5   C. 6   D. 6½

12._____

13. The difference in the cost of two typewriters is $56.64.
If the less expensive typewriter costs $307.22, what is the cost of the other typewriter?
A. $343.86   B. $344.06   C. $363.86   D. $364.06

13._____

14. At the start of a year, a family was receiving a public assistance grant of $382 twice a month, on the first and fifteenth of each month. On March 1, their rent allowance was decreased from $150 to $142 a month since they had moved to a smaller apartment. On August 1 their semi-monthly food allowance, which had been $80.40, was raised by 10%.
In that year, the TOTAL amount of money disbursed to this family was
A. $4,544.20   B. $6,581.40   C. $9,088.40   D. $9,168.40

14._____

15. It is discovered that a client has received double public assistance for 2 months by having been enrolled at two service centers of the Department of Social Services. The client should have received $168 twice a month instead of the double amount. He now agrees to repay the money by equal deductions from his public assistance check over a period of 12 months.
What will the amount of his NEXT check be?
A. $112 B. $140 C. $154 D. $160

16. Suppose a study is being made of the composition of 3,550 families receiving public assistance. Of the first 1,050 families reviewed, 18% had four or more children.
If, in the remaining number of families, the percentage with four or more children is half as high as the percentage in the group already reviewed, then the percentage of families with four or more children in the entire group of families is MOST NEARLY
A. 12 B. 14 C. 16 D. 17

17. Suppose that food prices have risen 13%, and an increase of the same amount has been granted in the food allotment given to people receiving public assistance.
If a family has been receiving $810 a month, 35% of which is allotted for food, then the TOTAL amount of public assistance this family receives per month will be changed to
A. $805.42 B. $840.06 C. $846.86 D. $899.42

18. Assume that the food allowance is to be raised 5% in August but will be retroactive for four months to April.
The retroactive allowance is to be divided into equal sections and added to the public assistance checks for August, September, October, November, and December.
A family which has been receiving $840 monthly, 40% of which was allotted for food, will receive what size check in August?
A. $853.44 B. $856.80 C. $861.00 D. $870.24

19. A blind client, who receives $210 public assistance twice a month, inherits 14 shares of stock worth $180 each. The client is required to sell the stock and spend his inheritance before receiving more public assistance.
Using his public assistance allowance as a guide, how many months are his new assets expected to last?
A. 6 B. 7 C. 8 D. 12

20. The Department of Social Services has 16 service centers. These centers may be divided into those which are downtown and those which are uptown. Two of the centers are special service centers and are downtown, while the remainder of the centers are general service centers. There is a total of 7 service centers downtown.
The percentage of the general service centers which are uptown is MOST NEARLY
A. 56 B. 64 C. 69 D. 79

21. For six months, a family lived in a 4-room apartment where they paid $380 a month. They made an intrasite move to a 4-room apartment where they paid $85 per room a month for six months.
Comparing the two six-month periods, the TOTAL amount of money the family saved by making the intrasite was
A. $240   B. $290   C. $430   D. $590

22. To calculate a tenant's usable income, you should make Social Security deductions of 4.4 percent on salary up to a maximum of $9,000 and State Disability deductions of .5 percent on salary up to $3,000.
What does a tenant's combined deduction amount to if his annual salary is $13,400?
A. $411.00   B. $568.60   C. $619.60   D. $700.00

23. If the temporary relocation expenses for housing are set at $18 per day for one adult and $10 per day for each additional person in a room, how much money is allowed for a woman and four children temporarily relocated in one room for a period of six days?
A. $168   B. $348   C. $378   D. $518

24. According to relocation policy, a family relocating to private housing from federally-aided or certain other sites will be granted a relocation payment. This payment equals the difference between 1/5 of the family's yearly income and the scheduled yearly rent for a standard apartment for their size family.
Suppose a 2-person family whose yearly income is $12,900 has been unable to obtain public housing and so finds a one-bedroom private apartment. The scheduled rent for a one-bedroom apartment appropriate for their occupancy is $240 a month.
What payment will they receive?
A. $240   B. $288   C. $300   D. $410

25. A family on a housing relocation site is paying $410 per month for rent. This represents 25% of their gross monthly income.
If the husband earns 4/5 of their total combined monthly income, how much does the wife earn per month?
A. $328   B. $540   C. $1,280   D. $1,500

KEY (CORRECT ANSWERS)

1.	A	11.	B
2.	B	12.	D
3.	C	13.	C
4.	B	14.	D
5.	B	15.	B
6.	A	16.	A
7.	C	17.	C
8.	C	18.	D
9.	A	19.	A
10.	D	20.	B

21. A
22. A
23. B
24. C
25. A

6 (#1)

SOLUTIONS TO PROBLEMS

1. After spring, the rent allotment should be $(240+24) = $264. After the summer, the reduced allotment for food and other necessities should be $[(280+140) − 1/7(280+140)] = $(420-1/7(420)] = $(420-60) = $360. The monthly check in the fall including rent, food, and other necessities should be $360 + $264 = $624.

2. Amount of general allowance in the family's semi-monthly check = $340. Amount of utilities allotment in the family's semi-monthly check: ($\frac{384}{12} \times ½$) = $16. Amount of general allowance in family' semi-monthly check after a 5% reduction = $340 less 5% of $340 = $(340-17) = $3223. Total amount of the next month's semi-monthly check: Reduced general allowance + utilities allotment = $323 + $16 = $339.

3. During 7 hours, a total of (15)(9) = 135 clients can be seen. Thus, in 35 hours, a total of (135)(5) = 675 clients will be seen.

4. 18(18+27) = .40 = 40%

5. $258.64 + $325.48 + $287.34 + $271.50 + $313.12 = $1,456.08

6. 4250/10 = 425 calls per day. Then, 425/17 = 25

7. (67+95+52+78+103)/5 = 79 hours

8. Number present = (240)(2/3) = 160

9. (25)(9) = 225 min. = 3 hrs. 45 min. = 3 ¾ hours

10. Let x, 1/4x = number of forms A, B, respectively. Then, x + 1/4x = 750. Solving, x = 600

11. $2,185.40 − (8)($156.10) = $936.60. Then, $936.60 ÷ $156.10 = 6 desks

12. Since the slow group did 12 folders each hour, the faster group did 24 folders each hour. Then, 234/(12+24) = 6 ½ hrs.

13. Expensive typewriter costs $307.22 + $56.64 = $363.86

14. For months of January and February, the amount the family receives is $(382×2×2) = $1528
    For months of March through July, the family receives $(764-8) × 5 = $3780
    For months August through December, the family receives $(756+16.08) × 5 = $3860.40
    The total amount of money disbursed to this family is $1528 + $3780 + $3860.40 = $9,168.40

15. The overpayment for 2 months = ($168)(4) = $672. If this is paid back over 12 months, each month's amount is reduced by $672/12 = $56. Then, each check (semi-monthly) is reduced by $28. His next check will be $168 - $28 = $140

7 (#1)

16. $(1050)(.18) + (2500)(.09) = 414$. Then, $414/3550 = 12\%$

17. $(\$810)(.35) = \$283.50$ originally allotted for food. The new food allotment = $(\$283.50)(1.13) = \$320.355$. The total assistance now = $\$810 - \$283.50 + \$320.355 = \$846.855$ or $\$846.86$

18. $(\$840)(.40) = \$336$ per month for food. The new food allowance = $(\$336)(1.05) = \$352.80$ per month. The difference of $16.80 is retroactive to April, which means $(\$16.80)(9) = \$151.20$ additional money for August through December. Each check for these 5 months will be increased by $15.20/5 = 30.24. Thus, the check in August = $840 + 30.24 = $840 + 30.24 = $870.24

19. $(\$180)(14) = \$2520$. Then, $\$2520/\$420 = 6$ months

20. 5 general are downtown; 9 of 14 general are uptown; $9/14 \approx 64\%$

21. $(\$85)(4) = \$340$ per month. Savings per month = $380 - $340 = $40 For six months, the savings = $240

22. $(\$9000(.044) + (\$3000)(.005) = \$411$ total deductions

23. $(\$18+\$40)(6) = \$348$ relocation expenses

24. $(\$240)(12) - (1/5)(\$12,900) = \$300$ relocation payment

25. $\$410 \div .25 = \$1640$. The wife earns $(1640)(1/5) = \$328$ each month

TEST 2

DIRECTIONS: Each question or incomplete statement is followed by several suggested answers or completions. Select the one that BEST answers the question or completes the statement. *PRINT THE LETTER OF THE CORRECT ANSWER IN THE SPACE AT THE RIGHT.*

1. A project tenant who owns and drives a taxicab for living, reports for a three-month period an income of $6,250 after operating expenses of $1,300 have been considered. In addition, his tips are valued at 12% of his income before operating expenses.
   An estimate of his yearly income is MOST NEARLY
   A. $22,000
   B. $23,000
   C. $28,000
   D. $28,500
   E. $29,000

2. The maximum annual subsidy which can be paid by the State toward the operation of any low-rent housing project is the sum of the annual interest on the total original loan or building the project and 1% of the portion of the loan actually spent.
   If the original loan for a project was $8,000,000 at 1¾% interest, but only $7,500,000 was actually spent, then the MAXIMUM annual subsidy is
   A. $140,000
   B. $145,000
   C. $215,000
   D. $220,000
   E. $271,250

3. In 2020, the cost of repairs and maintenance at a certain housing project was $5,589 more than in 2019, representing an increase of 4.6%. A further increase at the same rate was anticipated for 2021.
   The cost of repairs and maintenance in 2021 was MOST NEARLY
   A. $127,100
   B. $132,700
   C. $132,900
   D. $133,000
   E. an amount which cannot be determined from the given data

4. Each day a delivery truck used by the Housing Authority travels 25 miles from a project to a storehouse and 25 miles on the return trip. It travels at the rate of 30 miles per hour going to the storehouse and at the rate of 20 miles per hour returning.
   The average rate, in miles per hour, for the roundtrip is MOST NEARLY
   A. 24
   B. 25
   C. 26
   D. the square root of 600
   E. an amount which cannot be determined from the given data

5. A report on the first 6,000 applications for apartments in a certain project containing 1,400 apartments indicated that those who were ineligible fell into four categories: 2,800 ineligible for reason A, 600 ineligible for reason B, 1,200 ineligible for reason C, and 400 ineligible for reason D.

If the same proportions continue for the remaining 21,500 applications, then the percentage of eligible applicants who can be given apartments in the project is MOST NEARLY
A. 25   B. 30   C. 33   D. 40   E. 60

6. The number of applications for apartments in low-rent housing projects was 40,000 in 2019. The number of applications increased 5% in 2020, and increased again in 2021 by 6% over the 2,000 total.
The percentage by which the 2021 figures exceed the 2019 figures is
A. 5.3   B. 6.0   C. 11.0   D. 11.3   E. 30.0

6._____

7. A rectangular lot, 75 feet by 11.0 feet, was purchased as part of a project site for $28,500.
The price per square foot of this lot is MOST NEARLY
A. $2.85   B. $3.45   C. $3.95   D. $30.00   E. $30.95

7._____

8. It has been estimated that 125 kilowatt-hours of electricity are used each month in one average Housing Authority apartment at a cost of 14.8 cents per kilowatt-hour.
On this basis, the total cost of the electricity used in one year in a project containing 1,400 apartments is MOST NEARLY
A. $20,000   B. $25,000   C. $200,000
D. $250,000   E. $2,000,000

8._____

9. The walls and ceilings of 20 rooms are to be painted with the same kind of paint, each room being 15 feet long, 12 feet wide, and 10 feet high. Each room contains two windows, each 3 feet by 6 feet, and a door 3 feet by 8 feet, which are not to be painted. One gallon of paint covers 400 square feet of surface.
The number of gallons of paint needed is MOST NEARLY
A. 33   B. 34   C. 35   D. 36   E. 75

9._____

10. A group of buildings is valued at $11,500,000. Assume that the cos of fire insurance for these buildings is 5.3 cents per $100 of valuation per year.
The cost of fire insurance for one year is MOST NEARLY
A. $600   B. $6,000   C. $20,000
D. $60,000   E. $2,000,000

10._____

11. Of the 15 employees in a certain unit, one-third earn $27,600 per year, three earn $32,600, one earns $46,400, and the rest earn $33,800.
The average salary of the employees of this unit is MOST NEARLY
A. $31,000   B. $32,000   C. $33,000   D. $34,000   E. $35,000

11._____

12. Four pieces, each 2'8½" long, are cut from a piece of pipe 16½' long.
The length of the remaining piece of pipe is
A. 6'8½"   B. 6'10"   C. 6'10³/₈"   D. 6'11¹/₈"   E. 9'9½"

12._____

13. A tenant ears E dollars a month, spends S dollars a week, and saves the rest. The tenant's yearly savings can be expressed by
    A. 12(E-4S)   B. 12E – 52S   C. 12(E-S)
    D. 52(E-4S)   E. E - S

14. A unit of fifteen Housing Assistants has been assigned the job of interviewing applicants. Each interview takes 35 minutes, and an additional 10 minutes is needed for making entries and notes. The last interview each day is always scheduled so that it can be completed that day.
    The number of applicants who can be interviewed in a week, consisting of five 7-hour days, is MOST NEARLY
    A. 375   B. 525   C. 675   D. 700   E. 725

15. A review of the 14,000 applications for apartments in a certain project containing 1,200 apartments indicated that 4,800 applicants were eligible and 6,400 were ineligible. No decision could be reached on the remaining applications because certain necessary information was omitted by the applicants, but it was assumed that the proportion of eligible and ineligible applicants would remain the same as in those already decided.
    On the basis of these figures, the percentage of eligible applicants who can be given apartments in the project is
    A. under 17%   B. 17%   C. 20%
    D. 25%   E. 33 1/3%

16. An oil burner in a housing development burns 76 gallons of fuel oil per hour. At 9 A.M. on a very cold day, the superintendent asks the Housing Manager to put in an emergency order for more fuel oil. At that time, he reports that he has on hand 266 gallons. At noon, he again comes to the manager, notifying him that no oil has been delivered.
    The MAXIMUM amount of time that he can continue to furnish heat without receiving more oil is
    A. no more time   B. ½ hour   C. 1 hour
    D. 1½ hours   E. 2 hours

17. As a result of reports received by the Housing Authority concerning the reputed ineligibility of 756 tenants because of above-standard incomes, an intensive check of their employers has been ordered. Four housing assistants have been assigned to this task. At the end of 6 days at 7 hours each, they have checked on 336 tenants. In order to speed up the investigation, two more housing assistants are assigned to this point.
    If they worked at the same rate, the number of additional 7-hour days it would take to complete the job is MOST NEARLY
    A. 1   B. 3   C. 5   D. 7   E. 9

18. A municipal aide on a special trip is returning to his office from a point 17½ miles away, and makes the return trip to his office at an average speed of 25 miles an hour, except for a 15-minute stopover at one point to get a flat tire fixed. The time it should take him to reach his office is MOST NEARLY _____ minutes.
    A. 12   B. 22   C. 36   D. 42   E. 57

19. A district office has an assigned staff of 320 employees. Of this number, 25% are not available for duty due to illness, vacations, and other reasons. Of those who are available for duty, 1/8 are assigned to auditing and special projects, and the rest to handling the workload.
    The ACTUAL number of employees available for handling the workload is
    A. 350   B. 310   C. 270   D. 210   E. 180

20. Two dozen shuttlecocks and four badminton rackets are to be purchased for a playground. The shuttlecocks are priced at $3.60 each, and the rackets at $27.50 each. The playground receives a discount of 30% from these prices.
    The TOTAL cost of this equipment is
    A. $72.90   B. $114.30   C. $137.48   D. $186.00   E. $220.70

21. On January 1, a family was receiving public assistance allowance of $185 for food, $53 for clothing, $17.50 for utilities, and $22 for personal needs, all semi-monthly, and a monthly allowance of $550 for rent. On May 1, the rent allowance was increased by 12% but all other allowances remained the same for the rest of the year.
    The TOTAL amount of money granted this family during the year was
    A. $10,528   B. $13,262   C. $13,788
    D. $21,056   E. $27,676

22. It has been decided to make changes in food allotments to clients receiving public assistance to conform to changes in food costs. Of the food allowance, 30% is intended for meat, 30% for fruits and vegetables, 25% for groceries, and 15% for dairy products. Assume that meat prices have gone up 5%, and dairy prices have remained the same.
    For a family that has been receiving $400 per month for food, the new monthly food allowance will be
    A. $333   B. $375   C. $393   D. $403.50   E. $420

23. On January 1, a family was receiving a public assistance allowance of $195 for food, $63 for clothing, $27.50 for utilities, and $32 for personal needs, all semi-monthly, and a monthly allowance of $510 for rent. On June 1, the rent allowance was increased by 12%, but all other allowances remained the same for the rest of the year.
    The TOTAL amount of money granted this family during the year was
    A. $13,843.40   B. $14,107.20   C. $14,168.40
    D. $14,474.40   E. $16,886.80

5 (#2)

24. A member of a family receiving public assistance amounting to $600 monthly has obtained a part-time job, for which he is paid $40 a day. He is employed 3 days a week. His carfare costs $3.00 per day and his lunches $2.00 per day. Assume that there are $4^1/_3$ weeks per month. The Department of Welfare requires that net earnings be deducted from relief allowances.
The family's semi-monthly public assistance allowances should be reduced to
   A. $40.00   B. $72.50   C. $96.25   D. $123.75   E. $145.00

24.____

25. A couple living in a furnished room has been receiving a public assistance grant of $375 semi-monthly and has been paying a weekly rent of $75. The landlord has been granted a 12% increase in rent. Assume that a month consists of $4^1/_3$ weeks.
The amount of the new semi-monthly grant, including this rent increase, that the couple will receive will be MOST NEARLY
   A. $394.50   B. $397   C. $409   D. $514   E. $557

25.____

KEY (CORRECT ANSWERS)

1.	D		11.	B
2.	C		12.	A
3.	C		13.	B
4.	A		14.	C
5.	B		15.	C
6.	D		16.	B
7.	B		17.	C
8.	D		18.	E
9.	A		19.	D
10.	B		20.	C

21.	C
22.	C
23.	C
24.	B
25.	A

SOLUTIONS TO PROBLEMS

1. For 3 months, income = $6,250 + (.12)($7550) = $7156. Then, annual income = ($7154)(4) = $28,624, closest to $28,500.

2. Maximum annual subsidy = ($8,000,000)(.0175) + (.01)($7,500,000) = $215,000

3. Cost in 2019 = $5589/.046 = $121,500. The cost in 2020 = $121,500 + $5589 = $127,089. This means the cost in 2021 = ($127,089)(1.046) = $132,900

4. Average rate = total distance/total time = (25+25) ÷ (25/30 + 25/20) = 24 mph

5. Out of 600, number of eligible = 6000 – 2800 – 600 – 1200 – 400 = 1000. Thus, for 27,500 applications, (1/6)(27,500) = 4583 would be eligible. Finally, 1400 ÷ 4583 ≈ 30%

6. Number of applications in 2020 = (40,000)(1.05) = 42,000. Number of applications in 2021 = (42,000)(1.06) = 44,520. Then, (44,520–40,000) ÷ 40,000 = 11.3%

7. $28,500 ÷ [(75×110)] = $3.45 per sq. ft.

8. Total cost = (125)(.148)(12)(1400) = $310,800; closest to choice D of $250,000

9. Painted area of each room = (2)(15)(10) + (2)(12)(10) + (15)(12) – (2)(3)(6) – (3)(8) = 660 sq. ft. So, (20)(660) = 13,200 sq. ft. to be painted in all rooms. Finally, 13,200/400 = 33 gallons of paint needed

10. Insurance cost = (.053)($11,500,000)/$100 = $6095, closest to $6000

11. [(5)($27,600) + (3)($32,600) + (1)($46,400) + (6)($33,800)]/15 = $32,233 closest to $32,000

12. 16½ - (4)(2'5³/₈") = 16'6" – 8'21½" = 16'6" – 9'9½" = 6'8½"

13. Annual savings = 12E – 52S

14. 7 ÷ ¾ = $9.\overline{3}$, which means each interviewer can interview a maximum of 9 applicants each day. Then, (5)(9)(15) = 675 applicants

15. 4800/(4800+6400) = 3/7 eligible. On that assumption, there would be (3/7)(14,000) = 6000 eligible applicants. Then, 1200/6000 = 20%

16. 266 – (3)(76) = 38 gallons of oil left. Then, 38/76 = ½ hour

17. (6)(7)(4) = 168 hours to check on 336 tenants. This means 2 tenants require 1 man-hour. Now, (6)(7)(x days) = man-hours would be needed to check the remaining 420 tenants. This requires 210 man-hours. So, (6)(7)(x) = 210. Solving, x = 5

18. $\frac{17.5}{25}$ = .7 hr. = 42 min. Total time = 42 + 15 = 57 minutes.

7 (#2)

19. Number available = 320[1−.25(1/8)(.75) = 210

20. Total cost = (.70)[(24)($3.60)+(4)(27.50)] = $137.48

21. From January through April, amount = (8)($185+$53+$17.50+$22) + (4)($550) = $4420. From May through December, amount = (16)($185+$53+17.50+$22) + (8)($550)(1.12) = $9368. Total annual amount = $4420 + $9368 = $13,788

22. Meat allowance = ($400)(.30)(1.10) = $132; fruit and vegetable allowance = ($400)(.30)(.80) = $96; grocery allowance = ($400)(.25)(1.05) = $105; dairy allowance = ($400)(.15) = $60. New monthly allowance = $132 + $96 + $105 + $.60 = $393

23. From January through May, amount = (10)($195+$63+$27.50+$32) + (5)($510) = $5725. From June through December, amount = (14)($195+$63+$27.50+$32) + (7)($510)(1.12) = $8443.40. Total annual amount = $5725 + $8443.40 = $14,168.40

24. Monthly assistance should be reduced to $600 − [(40)(3)($4^{1}/_{3}$) − ($5)(3)($4^{1}/_{3}$)] = $145. So, the semi-monthly amount is now $145/2 = $72.50

25. ($75)($4^{1}/_{3}$)/2 = original semi-monthly rent.
New semi-monthly rent = (162.50)(1.12) = $182. Since this represents an increase of $19.50, the new semi-monthly grant will be increased to $375 + $19.50 = $394.50

PREPARING WRITTEN MATERIAL
EXAMINATION SECTION
TEST 1

DIRECTIONS: Each of the sentences in this test may be classified under one of the following four categories:
- A. Faulty because of incorrect grammar or word usage
- B. Faulty because of incorrect punctuation
- C. Faulty because of incorrect capitalization or incorrect spelling
- D. Correct

Examine each sentence carefully to determine under which of the above four options it is best classified. Then, in the space to the right, print the capital letter preceding the option which is the BEST of the four suggested above. (Note that each faulty sentence contains but one type of error. Consider a sentence to be correct if it contains none of the types of errors mentioned, even though there may be other correct ways of expressing the same thought.)

1. He sent the notice to the clerk who you hired yesterday.   1.____

2. It must be admitted, however that you were not informed of this change.   2.____

3. Only the employee who have served in this grade for at least two years are eligible for promotion.   3.____

4. The work was divided equally between she and Mary.   4.____

5. He thought that you were not available at that time.   5.____

6. When the messenger returns; please give him this package.   6.____

7. The new secretary prepared, typed, addressed, and delivered, the notices.   7.____

8. Walking into the room, his desk can be seen at the rear.   8.____

9. Although John has worked here longer than She, he produces a smaller amount of work.   9.____

10. She said she could of typed this report yesterday.   10.____

11. Neither one of these procedures are adequate for the efficient performance of this task.   11.____

12. The typewriter is the tool of the typist; the cash register, the tool of the cashier.   12.____

2 (#1)

13. "The assignment must be completed as soon as possible" said the supervisor. 13.____

14. As you know, office handbooks are issued to all new Employees. 14.____

15. Writing a speech is sometimes easier than to deliver it before an audience. 15.____

16. Mr. Brown our accountant, will audit the accounts next week. 16.____

17. Give the assignment to whomever is able to do it most efficiently. 17.____

18. The supervisor expected either your or I to file these reports. 18.____

KEY (CORRECT ANSWERS)

1.	A	11.	A
2.	B	12.	C
3.	D	13.	B
4.	A	14.	C
5.	D	15.	A
6.	B	16.	B
7.	B	17.	A
8.	A	18.	A
9.	C		
10.	A		

TEST 2

DIRECTIONS: Each of the sentences in this test may be classified under one of the following four categories:
  A. Faulty because of incorrect grammar or word usage
  B. Faulty because of incorrect punctuation
  C. Faulty because of incorrect capitalization or incorrect spelling
  D. Correct

Examine each sentence carefully to determine under which of the above four options it is best classified. Then, in the space to the right, print the capital letter preceding the option which is the BEST of the four suggested above. (Note that each faulty sentence contains but one type of error. Consider a sentence to be correct if it contains none of the types of errors mentioned, even though there may be other correct ways of expressing the same thought.)

1. The fire apparently started in the storeroom, which is usually locked.   1.____
2. On approaching the victim, two bruises were noticed by this officer.   2.____
3. The officer, who was there examined the report with great care.   3.____
4. Each employee in the office had a seperate desk.   4.____
5. All employees including members of the clerical staff, were invited to the lecture.   5.____
6. The suggested Procedure is similar to the one now in use.   6.____
7. No one was more pleased with the new procedure than the chauffeur.   7.____
8. He tried to persaude her to change the procedure.   8.____
9. The total of the expenses charged to petty cash were high.   9.____
10. An understanding between him and I was finally reached.   10.____

KEY (CORRECT ANSWERS)

1. D   6. C
2. A   7. D
3. B   8. C
4. C   9. A
5. B   10. A

TEST 3

DIRECTIONS: Each of the sentences in this test may be classified under one of the following four categories:
- A. Faulty because of incorrect grammar or word usage
- B. Faulty because of incorrect punctuation
- C. Faulty because of incorrect capitalization or incorrect spelling
- D. Correct

Examine each sentence carefully to determine under which of the above four options it is best classified. Then, in the space to the right, print the capital letter preceding the option which is the BEST of the four suggested above. (Note that each faulty sentence contains but one type of error. Consider a sentence to be correct if it contains none of the types of errors mentioned, even though there may be other correct ways of expressing the same thought.)

1. They told both he and I that the prisoner had escaped.   1.____

2. Any superior officer, who, disregards the just complaint of his subordinates, is remiss in the performance of his duty.   2.____

3. Only those members of the national organization who resided in the Middle West attended the conference in Chicago.   3.____

4. We told him to give the national organization assignment to whoever was available.   4.____

5. Please do not disappoint and embarass us by not appearing in court.   5.____

6. Although the office's speech proved to be entertaining, the topic was not relevent to the main theme of the conference.   6.____

7. In February all new officers attended a training course in which they were learned in their principal duties and the fundamental operating procedure of the department.   7.____

8. I personally seen inmate Jones threaten inmates Smith and Green with bodily harm if they refused to participate in the plot.   8.____

9. To the layman, who on a chance visit to the prison observes everything functioning smoothly, the maintenance of prison discipline may seem to be a relatively easily realizable objective.   9.____

10. The prisoners in cell block fourty were forbidden to sit on the cell cots during the recreation hour.   10.____

KEY (CORRECT ANSWERS)

1. A
2. B
3. C
4. D
5. C

6. C
7. A
8. A
9. D
10. C

TEST 4

DIRECTIONS: Each of the sentences in this test may be classified under one of the following four categories:
- A. Faulty because of incorrect grammar or word usage
- B. Faulty because of incorrect punctuation
- C. Faulty because of incorrect capitalization or incorrect spelling
- D. Correct

Examine each sentence carefully to determine under which of the above four options it is best classified. Then, in the space to the right, print the capital letter preceding the option which is the BEST of the four suggested above. (Note that each faulty sentence contains but one type of error. Consider a sentence to be correct if it contains none of the types of errors mentioned, even though there may be other correct ways of expressing the same thought.)

1. I cannot encourage you any. 1._____
2. You always look well in those sort of clothes. 2._____
3. Shall we go to the park? 3._____
4. The man whome he introduced was Mr. Carey. 4._____
5. She saw the letter laying here this morning. 5._____
6. It should rain before the Afternoon is over. 6._____
7. They have already went home. 7._____
8. That Jackson will be elected is evident. 8._____
9. He does not hardly approve of us. 9._____
10. It was he, who won the prize. 10._____

KEY (CORRECT ANSWERS)

1.	A	6.	C
2.	A	7.	A
3.	D	8.	D
4.	C	9.	A
5.	A	10.	B

TEST 5

DIRECTIONS: Each of the sentences in this test may be classified under one of the following four categories:
  A. Faulty because of incorrect grammar or word usage
  B. Faulty because of incorrect punctuation
  C. Faulty because of incorrect capitalization or incorrect spelling
  D. Correct

Examine each sentence carefully to determine under which of the above four options it is best classified. Then, in the space to the right, print the capital letter preceding the option which is the BEST of the four suggested above. (Note that each faulty sentence contains but one type of error. Consider a sentence to be correct if it contains none of the types of errors mentioned, even though there may be other correct ways of expressing the same thought.)

1. Shall we go to the park.   1.____
2. They are, alike, in this particular way.   2.____
3. They gave the poor man sume food when he knocked on the door.   3.____
4. I regret the loss caused by the error.   4.____
5. The students' will have a new teacher.   5.____
6. They sweared to bring out all the facts.   6.____
7. He decided to open a branch store on 33rd street.   7.____
8. His speed is equal and more than that of a racehorse.   8.____
9. He felt very warm on that Summer day.   9.____
10. He was assisted by his friend, who lives in the next house.   10.____

KEY (CORRECT ANSWERS)

1.	B	6.	A
2.	B	7.	C
3.	C	8.	A
4.	D	9.	C
5.	B	10.	D

TEST 6

DIRECTIONS: Each of the sentences in this test may be classified under one of the following four categories:
- A. Faulty because of incorrect grammar or word usage
- B. Faulty because of incorrect punctuation
- C. Faulty because of incorrect capitalization or incorrect spelling
- D. Correct

Examine each sentence carefully to determine under which of the above four options it is best classified. Then, in the space to the right, print the capital letter preceding the option which is the BEST of the four suggested above. (Note that each faulty sentence contains but one type of error. Consider a sentence to be correct if it contains none of the types of errors mentioned, even though there may be other correct ways of expressing the same thought.)

1. The climate of New York is colder than California. 1._____
2. I shall wait for you on the corner. 2._____
3. Did we see the boy who, we think, is the leader. 3._____
4. Being a modest person, John seldom talks about his invention. 4._____
5. The gang is called the smith street bos. 5._____
6. He seen the man break into the store. 6._____
7. We expected to lay still there for quite a while. 7._____
8. He is considered to be the Leader of his organization. 8._____
9. Although I recieved an invitation, I won't go. 9._____
10. The letter must be here some place. 10._____

KEY (CORRECT ANSWERS)

1.	A	6.	A
2.	D	7.	A
3.	B	8.	C
4.	D	9.	C
5.	C	10.	A

TEST 7

DIRECTIONS: Each of the sentences in this test may be classified under one of the following four categories:
- A. Faulty because of incorrect grammar or word usage
- B. Faulty because of incorrect punctuation
- C. Faulty because of incorrect capitalization or incorrect spelling
- D. Correct

Examine each sentence carefully to determine under which of the above four options it is best classified. Then, in the space to the right, print the capital letter preceding the option which is the BEST of the four suggested above. (Note that each faulty sentence contains but one type of error. Consider a sentence to be correct if it contains none of the types of errors mentioned, even though there may be other correct ways of expressing the same thought.)

1. I though it to be he.   1.____
2. We expect to remain here for a long time.   2.____
3. The committee was agreed.   3.____
4. Two-thirds of the building are finished.   4.____
5. The water was froze.   5.____
6. Everyone of the salesmen must supply their own car.   6.____
7. Who is the author of Gone With the Wind?   7.____
8. He marched on and declaring that he would never surrender.   8.____
9. Who shall I say called?   9.____
10. Everyone has left but they.   10.____

KEY (CORRECT ANSWERS)

1.	A	6.	A
2.	D	7.	B
3.	D	8.	A
4.	A	9.	D
5.	A	10.	D

TEST 8

DIRECTIONS: Each of the sentences in this test may be classified under one of the following four categories:
- A. Faulty because of incorrect grammar or word usage
- B. Faulty because of incorrect punctuation
- C. Faulty because of incorrect capitalization or incorrect spelling
- D. Correct

Examine each sentence carefully to determine under which of the above four options it is best classified. Then, in the space to the right, print the capital letter preceding the option which is the BEST of the four suggested above. (Note that each faulty sentence contains but one type of error. Consider a sentence to be correct if it contains none of the types of errors mentioned, even though there may be other correct ways of expressing the same thought.)

1. Who did we give the order to? 1._____
2. Send your order in immediately. 2._____
3. I believe I paid the Bill. 3._____
4. I have not met but one person. 4._____
5. Why aren't Tom, and Fred, going to the dance? 5._____
6. What reason is there for him not going? 6._____
7. The seige of Malta was a tremendous event. 7._____
8. I was there yesterday I assure you 8._____
9. Your ukulele is better than mine. 9._____
10. No one was there only Mary. 10._____

KEY (CORRECT ANSWERS)

1.	A	6.	A
2.	D	7.	C
3.	C	8.	B
4.	A	9.	C
5.	B	10.	A

TEST 9

DIRECTIONS: In each of the following groups of sentences, one of the four sentences is faulty in grammar, punctuation, or capitalization. Select the INCORRECT sentence in each case.

1. A. If you had stood at home and done your homework, you would not have failed in arithmetic.
   B. Her affected manner annoyed every member of the audience.
   C. How will the new law affect our income taxes?
   D. The plants were not affected by the long, cold winter, but they succumbed to the drought of summer.

   1.____

2. A. He is one of the most able men who have been in the Senate.
   B. It is he who is to blame for the lamentable mistake.
   C. Haven't you a helpful suggestion to make at this time?
   D. The money was robbed from the blind man's cup.

   2.____

3. A. The amount of children in this school is steadily increasing.
   B. After taking an apple from the table, she went out to play.
   C. He borrowed a dollar from me.
   D. I had hoped my brother would arrive before me.

   3.____

4. A. Whom do you think I hear from every week?
   B. Who do you think is the right man for the job?
   C. Who do you think I found in the room?
   D. He is the man whom we considered a good candidate for the presidency.

   4.____

5. A. Quietly the puppy laid down before the fireplace.
   B. You have made your bed; now lie in it.
   C. I was badly sunburned because I had lain too long in the sun.
   D. I laid the doll on the bed and left the room.

   5.____

KEY (CORRECT ANSWERS)

1. A
2. D
3. A
4. C
5. A

PHILOSOPHY, PRINCIPLES, PRACTICES, AND TECHNICS OF SUPERVISION, ADMINISTRATION, MANAGEMENT, AND ORGANIZATION

TABLE OF CONTENTS

	Page
MEANING OF SUPERVISION	1
THE OLD AND THE NEW SUPERVISION	1
THE EIGHT (8) BASIC PRINCIPLES OF THE NEW SUPERVISION	1
I. Principle of Responsibility	1
II. Principle of Authority	2
III. Principle of Self-Growth	2
IV. Principle of Individual Worth	2
V. Principle of Creative Leadership	2
VI. Principle of Success and Failure	2
VII. Principle of Science	3
VIII. Principle of Cooperation	3
WHAT IS ADMINISTRATION?	3
I. Practices Commonly Classed as "Supervisory"	3
II. Practices Commonly Classed as "Administrative"	3
III. Practices Commonly Classed as Both "Supervisory" and "Administrative"	4
RESPONSIBILITIES OF THE SUPERVISOR	4
COMPETENCIES OF THE SUPERVISOR	4
THE PROFESSIONAL SUPERVISOR-EMPLOYEE RELATIONSHIP	4
MINI-TEXT IN SUPERVISION, ADMINISTRATION, MANAGEMENT, AND ORGANIZATION	5
I. Brief Highlights	5
A. Levels of Management	6
B. What the Supervisor Must Learn	6
C. A Definition of Supervision	6
D. Elements of the Team Concept	6
E. Principles of Organization	6
F. The Four Important Parts of Every Job	7
G. Principles of Delegation	7
H. Principles of Effective Communications	7
I. Principles of Work Improvement	7
J. Areas of Job Improvement	7
K. Seven Key Points in Making Improvements	8

	L.	Corrective Techniques for Job Improvement	8
	M.	A Planning Checklist	8
	N.	Five Characteristics of Good Directions	9
	O.	Types of Directions	9
	P.	Controls	9
	Q.	Orienting the New Employee	9
	R.	Checklist for Orienting New Employees	9
	S.	Principles of Learning	10
	T.	Causes of Poor Performance	10
	U.	Four Major Steps in On-the-Job Instructions	10
	V.	Employees Want Five Things	10
	W.	Some Don'ts in Regard to Praise	11
	X.	How to Gain Your Workers' Confidence	11
	Y.	Sources of Employee Problems	11
	Z.	The Supervisor's Key to Discipline	11
	AA.	Five Important Processes of Management	12
	BB.	When the Supervisor Fails to Plan	12
	CC.	Fourteen General Principles of Management	12
	DD.	Change	12
II.	Brief Topical Summaries		13
	A.	Who/What is the Supervisor?	13
	B.	The Sociology of Work	13
	C.	Principles and Practices of Supervision	14
	D.	Dynamic Leadership	14
	E.	Processes for Solving Problems	15
	F.	Training for Results	15
	G.	Health, Safety, and Accident Prevention	16
	H.	Equal Employment Opportunity	16
	I.	Improving Communications	16
	J.	Self-Development	17
	K.	Teaching and Training	17
		1. The Teaching Process	17
		a. Preparation	17
		b. Presentation	18
		c. Summary	18
		d. Application	18
		e. Evaluation	18
		2. Teaching Methods	18
		a. Lecture	18
		b. Discussion	18
		c. Demonstration	19
		d. Performance	19
		e. Which Method to Use	19

PHILOSOPHY, PRINCIPLES, PRACTICES, AND TECHNICS OF SUPERVISION, ADMINISTRATION, MANAGEMENT, AND ORGANIZATION

MEANING OF SUPERVISION

The extension of the democratic philosophy has been accompanied by an extension in the scope of supervision. Modern leaders and supervisors no longer think of supervision in the narrow sense of being confined chiefly to visiting employees, supplying materials, or rating the staff. They regard supervision as being intimately related to all the concerned agencies of society, they speak of the supervisor's function in terms of "growth," rather than the "improvement" of employees.

This modern concept of supervision may be defined as follows: Supervision is leadership and the development of leadership within groups which are cooperatively engaged in inspection, research, training, guidance, and evaluation.

THE OLD AND THE NEW SUPERVISION

TRADITIONAL
1. Inspection
2. Focused on the employee
3. Visitation
4. Random and haphazard
5. Imposed and authoritarian
6. One person usually

MODERN
1. Study and analysis
2. Focused on aims, materials, methods, supervisors, employees, environment
3. Demonstrations, intervisitation, workshops, directed reading, bulletins, etc.
4. Definitely organized and planned (scientific)
5. Cooperative and democratic
6. Many persons involved (creative)

THE EIGHT (8) BASIC PRINCIPLES OF THE NEW SUPERVISION

I. Principle of Responsibility
   Authority to act and responsibility for acting must be joined.
   A. If you give responsibility, give authority.
   B. Define employee duties clearly.
   C. Protect employees from criticism by others.
   D. Recognize the rights as well as obligations of employees.
   E. Achieve the aims of a democratic society insofar as it is possible within the area of your work.
   F. Establish a situation favorable to training and learning.
   G. Accept ultimate responsibility for everything done in your section, unit, office, division, department.
   H. Good administration and good supervision are inseparable.

II. Principle of Authority
The success of the supervisor is measured by the extent to which the power of authority is not used.
   A. Exercise simplicity and informality in supervision
   B. Use the simplest machinery of supervision
   C. If it is good for the organization as a whole, it is probably justified.
   D. Seldom be arbitrary or authoritative.
   E. Do not base your work on the power of position or of personality.
   F. Permit and encourage the free expression of opinions.

III. Principle of Self-Growth
The success of the supervisor is measured by the extent to which, and the speed with which, he is no longer needed.
   A. Base criticism on principles, not on specifics.
   B. Point out higher activities to employees.
   C. Train for self-thinking by employees to meet new situations.
   D. Stimulate initiative, self-reliance, and individual responsibility
   E. Concentrate on stimulating the growth of employees rather than on removing defects.

IV. Principle of Individual Worth
Respect for the individual is a paramount consideration in supervision.
   A. Be human and sympathetic in dealing with employees.
   B. Don't nag about things to be done.
   C. Recognize the individual differences among employees and seek opportunities to permit best expression of each personality.

V. Principle of Creative Leadership
The best supervision is that which is not apparent to the employee.
   A. Stimulate, don't drive employees to creative action.
   B. Emphasize doing good things.
   C. Encourage employees to do what they do best.
   D. Do not be too greatly concerned with details of subject or method.
   E. Do not be concerned exclusively with immediate problems and activities.
   F. Reveal higher activities and make them both desired and maximally possible.
   G. Determine procedures in the light of each situation but see that these are derived from a sound basic philosophy.
   H. Aid, inspire, and lead so as to liberate the creative spirit latent in all good employees.

VI. Principle of Success and Failure
There are no unsuccessful employees, only unsuccessful supervisors who have failed to give proper leadership.
   A. Adapt suggestions to the capacities, attitudes, and prejudices of employees.
   B. Be gradual, be progressive, be persistent.
   C. Help the employee find the general principle; have the employee apply his own problem to the general principle.
   D. Give adequate appreciation for good work and honest effort.
   E. Anticipate employee difficulties and help to prevent them.
   F. Encourage employees to do the desirable things they will do anyway.
   G. Judge your supervision by the results it secures.

VII. Principle of Science
Successful supervision is scientific, objective, and experimental. It is based on facts, not on prejudices.
- A. Be cumulative in results.
- B. Never divorce your suggestions from the goals of training.
- C. Don't be impatient of results.
- D. Keep all matters on a professional, not a personal, level.
- E. Do not be concerned exclusively with immediate problems and activities.
- F. Use objective means of determining achievement and rating where possible.

VIII. Principle of Cooperation
Supervision is a cooperative enterprise between supervisor and employee.
- A. Begin with conditions as they are.
- B. Ask opinions of all involved when formulating policies.
- C. Organization is as good as its weakest link.
- D. Let employees help to determine policies and department programs.
- E. Be approachable and accessible—physically and mentally.
- F. Develop pleasant social relationships.

WHAT IS ADMINISTRATION

Administration is concerned with providing the environment, the material facilities, and the operational procedures that will promote the maximum growth and development of supervisors and employees. (Organization is an aspect and a concomitant of administration.)

There is no sharp line of demarcation between supervision and administration; these functions are intimately interrelated and, often, overlapping. They are complementary activities.

I. Practices Commonly Classed as "Supervisory"
- A. Conducting employees' conferences
- B. Visiting sections, units, offices, divisions, departments
- C. Arranging for demonstrations
- D. Examining plans
- E. Suggesting professional reading
- F. Interpreting bulletins
- G. Recommending in-service training courses
- H. Encouraging experimentation
- I. Appraising employee morale
- J. Providing for intervisitation

II. Practices Commonly Classified as "Administrative"
- A. Management of the office
- B. Arrangement of schedules for extra duties
- C. Assignment of rooms or areas
- D. Distribution of supplies
- E. Keeping records and reports
- F. Care of audio-visual materials
- G. Keeping inventory records
- H. Checking record cards and books

I.   Programming special activities
   J.   Checking on the attendance and punctuality of employees

III. Practices Commonly Classified as Both "Supervisory" and "Administrative"
   A.   Program construction
   B.   Testing or evaluating outcomes
   C.   Personnel accounting
   D.   Ordering instructional materials

RESPONSIBILITIES OF THE SUPERVISOR

A person employed in a supervisory capacity must constantly be able to improve his own efficiency and ability. He represent the employer to the employees and only continuous self-examination can make him a capable supervisor.

Leadership and training are the supervisor's responsibility. An efficient working unit is one in which the employees work with the supervisor. It is his job to bring out the best in his employees. He must always be relaxed, courteous, and calm in his association with his employees. Their feelings are important, and a harsh attitude does not develop the most efficient employees.

COMPETENCES OF THE SUPERVISOR

   I.   Complete knowledge of the duties and responsibilities of his position.
   II.   To be able to organize a job, plan ahead, and carry through.
   III. To have self-confidence and initiative.
   IV.   To be able to handle the unexpected situation and make quick decisions.
   V.   To be able to properly train subordinates in the positions they are best suited for.
   VI.   To be able to keep good human relations among his subordinates.
   VII. To be able to keep good human relations between his subordinates and himself and to earn their respect and trust.

THE PROFESSIONAL SUPERVISOR-EMPLOYEE RELATIONSHIP

There are two kinds of efficiency: one kind is only apparent and is produced in organizations through the exercise of mere discipline; this is but a simulation of the second, or true, efficiency which springs from spontaneous cooperation. If you are a manager, no matter how great or small your responsibility, it is your job, in the final analysis, to create and develop this involuntary cooperation among the people whom you supervise. For, no matter how powerful a combination of money, machines, and materials a company may have, this is a dead and sterile thing without a team of willing, thinking, and articulate people to guide it.

The following 21 points are presented as indicative of the exemplary basic relationship that should exist between supervisor and employee:

1. Each person wants to be liked and respected by his fellow employee and wants to be treated with consideration and respect by his superior.
2. The most competent employee will make an error. However, in a unit where good relations exist between the supervisor and his employees, tenseness and fear do not exist. Thus, errors are not hidden or covered up, and the efficiency of a unit is not impaired.

3. Subordinates resent rules, regulations, or orders that are unreasonable or unexplained.
4. Subordinates are quick to resent unfairness, harshness, injustices, and favoritism.
5. An employee will accept responsibility if he knows that he will be complimented for a job well done, and not too harshly chastised for failure; that his supervisor will check the cause of the failure, and, if it was the supervisor's fault, he will assume the blame therefore. If it was the employee's fault, his supervisor will explain the correct method or means of handling the responsibility.
6. An employee wants to receive credit for a suggestion he has made, that is used. If a suggestion cannot be used, the employee is entitled to an explanation. The supervisor should not say "no" and close the subject.
7. Fear and worry slow up a worker's ability. Poor working environment can impair his physical and mental health. A good supervisor avoids forceful methods, threats, and arguments to get a job done.
8. A forceful supervisor is able to train his employees individually and as a team, and is able to motivate them in the proper channels.
9. A mature supervisor is able to properly evaluate his subordinates and to keep them happy and satisfied.
10. A sensitive supervisor will never patronize his subordinates.
11. A worthy supervisor will respect his employees' confidences.
12. Definite and clear-cut responsibilities should be assigned to each executive.
13. Responsibility should always be coupled with corresponding authority.
14. No change should be made in the scope or responsibilities of a position without a definite understanding to that effect on the part of all persons concerned.
15. No executive or employee, occupying a single position in the organization, should be subject to definite orders from more than one source.
16. Orders should never be given to subordinates over the head of a responsible executive. Rather than do this, the officer in question should be supplanted.
17. Criticisms of subordinates should, whoever possible, be made privately, and in no case should a subordinate be criticized in the presence of executives or employees of equal or lower rank.
18. No dispute or difference between executives or employees as to authority or responsibilities should be considered too trivial for prompt and careful adjudication.
19. Promotions, wage changes, and disciplinary action should always be approved by the executive immediately superior to the one directly responsible.
20. No executive or employee should ever be required, or expected, to be at the same time an assistant to, and critic of, another.
21. Any executive whose work is subject to regular inspection should, wherever practicable, be given the assistance and facilities necessary to enable him to maintain an independent check of the quality of his work.

MINI-TEXT IN SUPERVISION, ADMINISTRATION, MANAGEMENT, AND ORGANIZATION

I. Brief Highlights

Listed concisely and sequentially are major headings and important data in the field for quick recall and review.

A. Levels of Management
Any organization of some size has several levels of management. In terms of a ladder, the levels are:

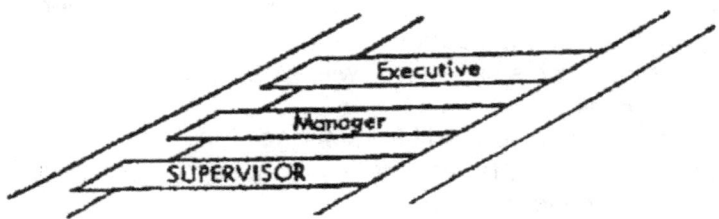

The first level is very important because it is the beginning point of management leadership.

B. What the Supervisor Must Learn
A supervisor must learn to:
1. Deal with people and their differences
2. Get the job done through people
3. Recognize the problems when they exist
4. Overcome obstacles to good performance
5. Evaluate the performance of people
6. Check his own performance in terms of accomplishment

C. A Definition of Supervisor
The term supervisor means any individual having authority, in the interests of the employer, to hire, transfer, suspend, lay-off, recall, promote, discharge, assign, reward, or discipline other employees or responsibility to direct them, or to adjust their grievances, or effectively to recommend such action, if, in connection with the foregoing, exercise of such authority is not of a merely routine or clerical nature but requires the use of independent judgment.

D. Elements of the Team Concept
What is involved in teamwork? The component parts are:
1. Members
2. A leader
3. Goals
4. Plans
5. Cooperation
6. Spirit

E. Principles of Organization
1. A team member must know what his job is.
2. Be sure that the nature and scope of a job are understood.
3. Authority and responsibility should be carefully spelled out.
4. A supervisor should be permitted to make the maximum number of decisions affecting his employees.
5. Employees should report to only one supervisor.
6. A supervisor should direct only as many employees as he can handle effectively.
7. An organization plan should be flexible.

8. Inspection and performance of work should be separate.
9. Organizational problems should receive immediate attention.
10. Assign work in line with ability and experience.

F. The Four Important Parts of Every Job
1. Inherent in every job is the *accountability* for results.
2. A second set of factors in every job is *responsibilities*.
3. Along with duties and responsibilities one must have the *authority* to act within certain limits without obtaining permission to proceed.
4. No job exists in a vacuum. The supervisor is surrounded by key *relationships*.

G. Principles of Delegation
Where work is delegated for the first time, the supervisor should think in terms of these questions:
1. Who is best qualified to do this?
2. Can an employee improve his abilities by doing this?
3. How long should an employee spend on this?
4. Are there any special problems for which he will need guidance?
5. How broad a delegation can I make?

H. Principles of Effective Communications
1. Determine the media.
2. To whom directed?
3. Identification and source authority.
4. Is communication understood?

I. Principles of Work Improvement
1. Most people usually do only the work which is assigned to them.
2. Workers are likely to fit assigned work into the time available to perform it.
3. A good workload usually stimulates output.
4. People usually do their best work when they know that results will be reviewed or inspected.
5. Employees usually feel that someone else is responsible for conditions of work, workplace layout, job methods, type of tools/equipment, and other such factors.
6. Employees are usually defensive about their job security.
7. Employees have natural resistance to change.
8. Employees can support or destroy a supervisor.
9. A supervisor usually earns the respect of his people through his personal example of diligence and efficiency.

J. Areas of Job Improvement
The areas of job improvement are quite numerous, but the most common ones which a supervisor can identify and utilize are:
1. Departmental layout
2. Flow of work
3. Workplace layout
4. Utilization of manpower
5. Work methods
6. Materials handling

7. Utilization
8. Motion economy

K. Seven Key Points in Making Improvements
1. Select the job to be improved
2. Study how it is being done now
3. Question the present method
4. Determine actions to be taken
5. Chart proposed method
6. Get approval and apply
7. Solicit worker participation

l. Corrective Techniques of Job Improvement
Specific Problems
1. Size of workload
2. Inability to meet schedules
3. Strain and fatigue
4. Improper use of men and skills
5. Waste, poor quality, unsafe conditions
6. Bottleneck conditions that hinder output
7. Poor utilization of equipment and machine
8. Efficiency and productivity of labor

General Improvement
1. Departmental layout
2. Flow of work
3. Work plan layout
4. Utilization of manpower
5. Work methods
6. Materials handling
7. Utilization of equipment
8. Motion economy

Corrective Techniques
1. Study with scale model
2. Flow chart study
3. Motion analysis
4. Comparison of units produced to standard allowance
5. Methods analysis
6. Flow chart and equipment study
7. Down time vs. running time
8. Motion analysis

M. A Planning Checklist
1. Objectives
2. Controls
3. Delegations
4. Communications
5. Resources
6. Manpower

7. Equipment
8. Supplies and materials
9. Utilization of time
10. Safety
11. Money
12. Work
13. Timing of improvements

N. Five Characteristics of Good Directions
In order to get results, directions must be:
1. Possible of accomplishment
2. Agreeable with worker interests
3. Related to mission
4. Planned and complete
5. Unmistakably clear

O. Types of Directions
1. Demands or direct orders
2. Requests
3. Suggestion or implication
4. volunteering

P. Controls
A typical listing of the overall areas in which the supervisor should establish controls might be:
1. Manpower
2. Materials
3. Quality of work
4. Quantity of work
5. Time
6. Space
7. Money
8. Methods

Q. Orienting the New Employee
1. Prepare for him
2. Welcome the new employee
3. Orientation for the job
4. Follow-up

R. Checklist for Orienting New Employees   Yes   No
1. Do you appreciate the feelings of new employees
   when they first report for work?   ___   ___
2. Are you aware of the fact that the new employee must
   make a big adjustment to his job?   ___   ___
3. Have you given him good reasons for liking the job and
   the organization?   ___   ___
4. Have you prepared for his first day on the job?   ___   ___
5. Did you welcome him cordially and make him feel needed?   ___   ___

		Yes	No
6.	Did you establish rapport with him so that he feels free to talk and discuss matters with you?	___	___
7.	Did you explain his job to him and his relationship to you?	___	___
8.	Does he know that his work will be evaluated periodically on a basis that is fair and objective?	___	___
9.	Did you introduce him to his fellow workers in such a way that they are likely to accept him?	___	___
10.	Does he know what employee benefits he will receive?	___	___
11.	Does he understand the importance of being on the job and what to do if he must leave his duty station?	___	___
12.	Has he been impressed with the importance of accident prevention and safe practice?	___	___
13.	Does he generally know his way around the department?	___	___
14.	Is he under the guidance of a sponsor who will teach the right way of doing things?	___	___
15.	Do you plan to follow-up so that he will continue to adjust successfully to his job?	___	___

S. Principles of Learning
   1. Motivation
   2. Demonstration or explanation
   3. Practice

T. Causes of Poor Performance
   1. Improper training for job
   2. Wrong tools
   3. Inadequate directions
   4. Lack of supervisory follow-up
   5. Poor communications
   6. Lack of standards of performance
   7. Wrong work habits
   8. Low morale
   9. Other

U. Four Major Steps in On-The-Job Instruction
   1. Prepare the worker
   2. Present the operation
   3. Tryout performance
   4. Follow-up

V. Employees Want Five Things
   1. Security
   2. Opportunity
   3. Recognition
   4. Inclusion
   5. Expression

W. Some Don'ts in Regard to Praise
1. Don't praise a person for something he hasn't done.
2. Don't praise a person unless you can be sincere.
3. Don't be sparing in praise just because your superior withholds it from you.
4. Don't let too much time elapse between good performance and recognition of it

X. How to Gain Your Workers' Confidence
Methods of developing confidence include such things as:
1. Knowing the interests, habits, hobbies of employees
2. Admitting your own inadequacies
3. Sharing and telling of confidence in others
4. Supporting people when they are in trouble
5. Delegating matters that can be well handled
6. Being frank and straightforward about problems and working conditions
7. Encouraging others to bring their problems to you
8. Taking action on problems which impede worker progress

Y. Sources of Employee Problems
On-the-job causes might be such things as:
1. A feeling that favoritism is exercised in assignments
2. Assignment of overtime
3. An undue amount of supervision
4. Changing methods or systems
5. Stealing of ideas or trade secrets
6. Lack of interest in job
7. Threat of reduction in force
8. Ignorance or lack of communications
9. Poor equipment
10. Lack of knowing how supervisor feels toward employee
11. Shift assignments

Off-the-job problems might have to do with:
1. Health
2. Finances
3. Housing
4. Family

Z. The Supervisor's Key to Discipline
There are several key points about discipline which the supervisor should keep in mind:
1. Job discipline is one of the disciplines of life and is directed by the supervisor.
2. It is more important to correct an employee fault than to fix blame for it.
3. Employee performance is affected by problems both on the job and off.
4. Sudden or abrupt changes in behavior can be indications of important employee problems.
5. Problems should be dealt with as soon as possible after they are identified.
6. The attitude of the supervisor may have more to do with solving problems than the techniques of problem solving.
7. Correction of employee behavior should be resorted to only after the supervisor is sure that training or counseling will not be helpful.

8. Be sure to document your disciplinary actions.
9. Make sure that you are disciplining on the basis of facts rather than personal feelings.
10. Take each disciplinary step in order, being careful not to make snap judgments, or decisions based on impatience.

AA. Five Important Processes of Management
1. Planning
2. Organizing
3. Scheduling
4. Controlling
5. Motivating

BB. When the Supervisor Fails to Plan
1. Supervisor creates impression of not knowing his job
2. May lead to excessive overtime
3. Job runs itself—supervisor lacks control
4. Deadlines and appointments missed
5. Parts of the work go undone
6. Work interrupted by emergencies
7. Sets a bad example
8. Uneven workload creates peaks and valleys
9. Too much time on minor details at expense of more important tasks

CC. Fourteen General Principles of Management
1. Division of work
2. Authority and responsibility
3. Discipline
4. Unity of command
5. Unity of direction
6. Subordination of individual interest to general interest
7. Remuneration of personnel
8. Centralization
9. Scalar chain
10. Order
11. Equity
12. Stability of tenure of personnel
13. Initiative
14. Esprit de corps

DD. Change

Bringing about change is perhaps attempted more often, and yet less well understood, than anything else the supervisor does. How do people generally react to change? (People tend to resist change that is imposed upon them by other individuals or circumstances.

Change is characteristic of every situation. It is a part of every real endeavor where the efforts of people are concerned.

1. Why do people resist change?
   People may resist change because of:
   a. Fear of the unknown
   b. Implied criticism
   c. Unpleasant experiences in the past
   d. Fear of loss of status
   e. Threat to the ego
   f. Fear of loss of economic stability

2. How can we best overcome the resistance to change?
   In initiating change, take these steps:
   a. Get ready to sell
   b. Identify sources of help
   c. Anticipate objections
   d. Sell benefits
   e. Listen in depth
   f. Follow up

II. Brief Topical Summaries

   A. Who/What is the Supervisor?
      1. The supervisor is often called the "highest level employee and the lowest level manager."
      2. A supervisor is a member of both management and the work group. He acts as a bridge between the two.
      3. Most problems in supervision are in the area of human relations, or people problems.
      4. Employees expect: Respect, opportunity to learn and to advance, and a sense of belonging, and so forth.
      5. Supervisors are responsible for directing people and organizing work. Planning is of paramount importance.
      6. A position description is a set of duties and responsibilities inherent to a given position.
      7. It is important to keep the position description up-to-date and to provide each employee with his own copy.

   B. The Sociology of Work
      1. People are alike in many ways; however, each individual is unique.
      2. The supervisor is challenged in getting to know employee differences. Acquiring skills in evaluating individuals is an asset.
      3. Maintaining meaningful working relationships in the organization is of great importance.
      4. The supervisor has an obligation to help individuals to develop to their fullest potential.
      5. Job rotation on a planned basis helps to build versatility and to maintain interest and enthusiasm in work groups.
      6. Cross training (job rotation) provides backup skills.

7. The supervisor can help reduce tension by maintaining a sense of humor, providing guidance to employees, and by making reasonable and timely decisions. Employees respond favorably to working under reasonably predictable circumstances.
8. Change is characteristic of all managerial behavior. The supervisor must adjust to changes in procedures, new methods, technological changes, and to a number of new and sometimes challenging situations.
9. To overcome the natural tendency for people to resist change, the supervisor should become more skillful in initiating change.

C. Principles and Practices of Supervision
1. Employees should be required to answer to only one superior.
2. A supervisor can effectively direct only a limited number of employees, depending upon the complexity, variety, and proximity of the jobs involved.
3. The organizational chart presents the organization in graphic form. It reflects lines of authority and responsibility as well as interrelationships of units within the organization.
4. Distribution of work can be improved through an analysis using the "Work Distribution Chart."
5. The "Work Distribution Chart" reflects the division of work within a unit in understandable form.
6. When related tasks are given to an employee, he has a better chance of increasing his skills through training.
7. The individual who is given the responsibility for tasks must also be given the appropriate authority to insure adequate results.
8. The supervisor should delegate repetitive, routine work. Preparation of recurring reports, maintaining leave and attendance records are some examples.
9. Good discipline is essential to good task performance. Discipline is reflected in the actions of employees on the job in the absence of supervision.
10. Disciplinary action may have to be taken when the positive aspects of discipline have failed. Reprimand, warning, and suspension are examples of disciplinary action.
11. If a situation calls for a reprimand, be sure it is deserved and remember it is to be done in private.

D. Dynamic Leadership
1. A style is a personal method or manner of exerting influence.
2. Authoritarian leaders often see themselves as the source of power and authority.
3. The democratic leader often perceives the group as the source of authority and power.
4. Supervisors tend to do better when using the pattern of leadership that is most natural for them.
5. Social scientists suggest that the effective supervisor use the leadership style that best fits the problem or circumstances involved.
6. All four styles—telling, selling, consulting, joining—have their place. Using one does not preclude using the other at another time.

7. The theory X point of view assumes that the average person dislikes work, will avoid it whenever possible, and must be coerced to achieve organizational objectives.
8. The theory Y point of view assumes that the average person considers work to be a natural as play, and, when the individual is committed, he requires little supervision or direction to accomplish desired objectives.
9. The leader's basic assumptions concerning human behavior and human nature affect his actions, decisions, and other managerial practices.
10. Dissatisfaction among employees is often present, but difficult to isolate. The supervisor should seek to weaken dissatisfaction by keeping promises, being sincere and considerate, keeping employees informed, and so forth.
11. Constructive suggestions should be encouraged during the natural progress of the work.

E. Processes for Solving Problems
1. People find their daily tasks more meaningful and satisfying when they can improve them.
2. The causes of problems, or the key factors, are often hidden in the background. Ability to solve problems often involves the ability to isolate them from their backgrounds. There is some substance to the cliché that some persons "can't see the forest for the trees."
3. New procedures are often developed from old ones. Problems should be broken down into manageable parts. New ideas can be adapted from old one.
4. People think differently in problem-solving situations. Using a logical, patterned approach is often useful. One approach found to be useful includes these steps:
   a. Define the problem
   b. Establish objectives
   c. Get the facts
   d. Weigh and decide
   e. Take action
   f. Evaluate action

F. Training for Results
1. Participants respond best when they feel training is important to them.
2. The supervisor has responsibility for the training and development of those who report to him.
3. When training is delegated to others, great care must be exercised to insure the trainer has knowledge, aptitude, and interest for his work as a trainer.
4. Training (learning) of some type goes on continually. The most successful supervisor makes certain the learning contributes in a productive manner to operational goals.
5. New employees are particularly susceptible to training. Older employees facing new job situations require specific training, as well as having need for development and growth opportunities.
6. Training needs require continuous monitoring.
7. The training officer of an agency is a professional with a responsibility to assist supervisors in solving training problems.

8. Many of the self-development steps important to the supervisor's own growth are equally important to the development of peers and subordinates. Knowledge of these is important when the supervisor consults with others on development and growth opportunities.

G. Health, Safety, and Accident Prevention
1. Management-minded supervisors take appropriate measures to assist employees in maintaining health and in assuring safe practices in the work environment.
2. Effective safety training and practices help to avoid injury and accidents.
3. Safety should be a management goal. All infractions of safety which are observed should be corrected without exception.
4. Employees' safety attitude, training and instruction, provision of safe tools and equipment, supervision, and leadership are considered highly important factors which contribute to safety and which can be influenced directly by supervisors.
5. When accidents do occur, they should be investigated promptly for very important reasons, including the fact that information which is gained can be used to prevent accidents in the future.

H. Equal Employment Opportunity
1. The supervisor should endeavor to treat all employees fairly, without regard to religion, race, sex, or national origin.
2. Groups tend to reflect the attitude of the leader. Prejudice can be detected even in very subtle form. Supervisors must strive to create a feeling of mutual respect and confidence in every employee.
3. Complete utilization of all human resources is a national goal. Equitable consideration should be accorded women in the work force, minority-group members, the physically and mentally handicapped, and the older employee. The important question is: "Who can do the job?"
4. Training opportunities, recognition for performance, overtime assignments, promotional opportunities, and all other personnel actions are to be handled on an equitable basis.

I. Improving Communications
1. Communications is achieving understanding between the sender and the receiver of a message. It also means sharing information—the creation of understanding.
2. Communication is basic to all human activity. Words are means of conveying meanings; however, real meanings are in people.
3. There are very practical differences in the effectiveness of one-way, impersonal, and two-way communications. Words spoken face-to-face are better understood. Telephone conversations are effective, but lack the rapport of person-to-person exchanges. The whole person communicates.
4. Cooperation and communication in an organization go hand in hand. When there is a mutual respect between people, spelling out rules and procedures for communicating is unnecessary.
5. There are several barriers to effective communications. These include failure to listen with respect and understanding, lack of skill in feedback, and misinterpreting the meanings of words used by the speaker. It is also common

practice to listen to what we want to hear, and tune out things we do not want to hear.
6. Communication is management's chief problem. The supervisor should accept the challenge to communicate more effectively and to improve interagency and intra-agency communications.
7. The supervisor may often plan for and conduct meetings. The planning phase is critical and may determine the success or the failure of a meeting.
8. Speaking before groups usually requires extra effort. Stage fright may never disappear completely, but it can be controlled.

J. Self-Development
1. Every employee is responsible for his own self-development.
2. Toastmaster and toastmistress clubs offer opportunities to improve skills in oral communications.
3. Planning for one's own self-development is of vital importance. Supervisors know their own strengths and limitations better than anyone else.
4. Many opportunities are open to aid the supervisor in his developmental efforts, including job assignments; training opportunities, both governmental and non-governmental—to include universities and professional conferences and seminars.
5. Programmed instruction offers a means of studying at one's own rate.
6. Where difficulties may arise from a supervisor's being away from his work for training, he may participate in televised home study or correspondence courses to meet his self-development needs.

K. Teaching and Training
1. The Teaching Process
Teaching is encouraging and guiding the learning activities of students toward established goals. In most cases this process consists of five steps: preparation, presentation, summarization, evaluation, and application.

   a. Preparation
   Preparation is two-fold in nature; that of the supervisor and the employee. Preparation by the supervisor is absolutely essential to success. He must know what, when, where, how, and whom he will teach. Some of the factors that should be considered are:
   1) The objectives
   2) The materials needed
   3) The methods to be used
   4) Employee participation
   5) Employee interest
   6) Training aids
   7) Evaluation
   8) Summarization

   Employee preparation consists in preparing the employee to receive the material. Probably the most important single factor in the preparation of the employee is arousing and maintaining his interest. He must know the objectives of the training, why he is there, how the material can be used, and its importance to him.

b. Presentation
In presentation, have a carefully designed plan and follow it. The plan should be accurate and complete, yet flexible enough to meet situations as they arise. The method of presentation will be determined by the particular situation and objectives.

c. Summary
A summary should be made at the end of every training unit and program. In addition, there may be internal summaries depending on the nature of the material being taught. The important thing is that the trainee must always be able to understand how each part of the new material relates to the whole.

d. Application
The supervisor must arrange work so the employee will be given a chance to apply new knowledge or skills while the material is still clear in his mind and interest is high. The trainee does not really know whether he has learned the material until he has been given a chance to apply it. If the material is not applied, it loses most of its value.

e. Evaluation
The purpose of all training is to promote learning. To determine whether the training has been a success or failure, the supervisor must evaluate this learning.
In the broadest sense, evaluation includes all the devices, methods, skills, and techniques used by the supervisor to keep himself and the employees informed as to their progress toward the objectives they are pursuing. The extent to which the employee has mastered the knowledge, skills, and abilities, or changed his attitudes, as determined by the program objectives, is the extent to which instruction has succeeded or failed.
Evaluation should not be confined to the end of the lesson, day, or program but should be used continuously. We shall note later the way this relates to the rest of the teaching process.

2. Teaching Methods
A teaching method is a pattern of identifiable student and instructor activity used in presenting training material.
All supervisors are faced with the problem of deciding which method should be used at a given time.

a. Lecture
The lecture is direct oral presentation of material by the supervisor. The present trend is to place less emphasis on the trainer's activity and more on that of the trainee.

b. Discussion
Teaching by discussion or conference involves using questions and other techniques to arouse interest and focus attention upon certain areas, and by doing so creating a learning situation. This can be one of the most

valuable methods because it gives the employees an opportunity to express their ideas and pool their knowledge.

    c. Demonstration
The demonstration is used to teach how something works or how to do something. It can be used to show a principle or what the results of a series of actions will be. A well-staged demonstration is particularly effective because it shows proper methods of performance in a realistic manner.

    d. Performance
Performance is one of the most fundamental of all learning techniques or teaching methods. The trainee may be able to tell how a specific operation should be performed but he cannot be sure he knows how to perform the operation until he has done so.
As with all methods, there are certain advantages and disadvantages to each method.

    e. Which Method to Use
Moreover, there are other methods and techniques of teaching. It is difficult to use any method without other methods entering into it. In any learning situation, a combination of methods is usually more effective than any one method alone.

Finally, evaluation must be integrated into the other aspects of the teaching-learning process.

It must be used in the motivation of the trainees; it must be used to assist in developing understanding during the training; and it must be related to employee application of the results of training.

This is distinctly the role of the supervisor.

www.ingramcontent.com/pod-product-compliance
Lightning Source LLC
Chambersburg PA
CBHW080322020526
44117CB00035B/2596